HOMESTEAD
SURVIVAL

HOMESTEAD SURVIVAL

An Insider's Guide to Your Great Escape

 **MARTY RANEY**

A TarcherPerigee Book

an imprint of Penguin Random House LLC
penguinrandomhouse.com

Library of Congress Cataloging-in-Publication Data

Names: Raney, Marty, author.
Title: Homestead survival: an insider's guide to your great escape / Marty Raney.
Other titles: Insider's guide to your great escape
Description: First edition | [New York]: TarcherPerigee, Penguin Random House LLC, [2022]
Identifiers: LCCN 2022005934 (print) | LCCN 2022005935 (ebook) |
ISBN 9780593420683 (trade paperback) | ISBN 9780593420690 (epub)
Subjects: LCSH: Wilderness survival—Handbooks, manuals, etc. | Frontier and pioneer life—Handbooks, manuals, etc. | Survivalism—Handbooks, manuals, etc. | Handbooks and manuals.
Classification: LCC GV200.5.R36 2022 (print) | LCC GV200.5 (ebook) | DDC 613.6/9—dc23/eng/20220225
LC record available at https://lccn.loc.gov/2022005934
LC ebook record available at https://lccn.loc.gov/2022005935

Printed in the United States
1st Printing

Book design by Shannon Nicole Plunkett

AUTHOR'S NOTE

At the beginning of the COVID-19 pandemic, an urban exodus began. Tens of millions of people began fleeing crowded, troubled cities in search of less stressful, healthier lives in the country. This book's mission is to successfully guide any and all down that path to a simpler, better life of self-sufficiency.

CONTENTS

INTRODUCTION

On the morning of November 30, 2018, I left our homestead in Hatcher Pass at eight o'clock to get building supplies. It was still dark, as the sun doesn't rise until about ten that time of year in Alaska. As I sat at a red light on the Parks Highway in downtown Wasilla, the earth began to ripple violently like waves on the water. Trees swayed, the ground moved, and I thought, "This might be the big one!" It was, by far, the biggest quake I'd ever felt (registering 7.2). Immediately after the quaking stopped, the power went out. And then, six minutes later, another 5.7 earthquake. Whoa. Police cars, fire trucks, and other aid vehicles with lights ablaze and sirens ablare sped in every direction.

I abandoned my mission to get supplies and immediately thought of those in my circle. I called my wife, Mollee, who said she was fine and planned to assess homestead damage once the sun came up. I then called my parents, but the line was dead. I turned my truck around and headed for their house. As I passed the grocery store, I saw hundreds of people crowded around the entrance, and it looked like they were being handed free bottled water. The huge plate glass window storefront was now lying on the concrete sidewalk in a million pieces, and the asphalt parking lot had a significant earthquake crack running at least fifty yards, straight into the building. Every gas station had a line of cars and trucks that backed up onto the main roads, and it was apparent this quake had caused certain damage and significant panic.

As I entered my parents' driveway, their powerless house was pitch-black. I walked in and found them sitting quietly in the dark, stranded in their respective well-worn recliners, surrounded by an ocean of broken glass. They were anxiously reliving the quake back to me as I scooped, swept, and vacuumed the dangerous debris. Once the glass was gone and my (amazing) mom had told me ten different illustrative versions of their crazy morning, I set off for my place.

On the fifteen-mile drive back to Hatcher Pass, I couldn't stop thinking about how ill-prepared everyone had been that morning. Not enough food. Not enough water. Not enough fuel. A few hours after the quake, every generator on every shelf had been purchased. Any store that was not damaged by the quake saw desperate throngs hoarding necessities.

———————————

Alaskans are well aware of the 9.2 earthquake of 1964, when the earth opened up and swallowed cars, houses, and buildings, killing 115 people. The adage "It's not over 'til it's over" is never more true than during an earthquake. When you and the ground you're standing on stop shaking, there's often more to come. There's also something far worse than a short-lived earthquake brewing in the ocean, and it's traveling at a minimum of 500 mph: a tsunami. Destination? The coastline. The quake of '64 triggered tsunami waves that devastated coastal villages and displaced huge fishing boats in Kodiak from their respective moorage slips to high and dry front yards. Thankfully the two big quakes back to back in 2018 didn't trigger a significant tsunami, and come sunrise people began to assess their commercial and residential damages. What did I take away from that earthshaking event? Simply this: No one was prepared.

Earthquakes are to Alaskans as tornadoes are to midwesterners. They're unpredictable, destructive, deadly, and common. Add to the mix hurricanes, ice storms, pandemics, cyberattacks on any and everything from fuel to food, water, and power sources, and, dare I say it, wars. There's never been more people on Planet Earth than now. There's never been more potential to harm said people than now. And there will never be a better time than right now to wake up and admit the cold hard facts. Hard times are here, harder times are on the horizon, and no one's prepared.

A RANEY DAY

Today, four years after the 7.2 earthquake, I still lead two not so distinctly different lives. One is my Alaskan life, where I work as a contractor while striving to live simply and self-sufficiently on a rugged, forty-acre homestead that has challenged me like no other. My second life finds me traversing North America, answering the calls of prospective homesteaders who have reached out to me for a helping hand with their own (seemingly insurmountable) challenges that they've encountered while pursuing a simpler life.

I've long lost track of how many properties, cabins, homes, and homesteads I've worked on—thousands, for sure. It seems like I got put to work on the day I was born, and from early on it's all I can remember. Work. But if any good can be said about my lifetime of hard-scrabble, it's this: It's given me a diverse skill set that qualifies me to travel anywhere to help anyone with anything. These two lives are inseparable. I work in Alaska to fulfill our family's dream to live freely, simply, self-sufficiently, independently, and closer to nature. I travel to assist others to do the same, helping them to fulfill *their* families' dreams, fueled by hope and their own respective principles, fundamentals, and beliefs. And as hats go, this one fits well. I can relate to their challenges and empathize with their frustrations. I live this unique lifestyle, although the less-traveled homesteading highway has its blind corners, hairpin turns, and ups and downs. However, there is no other lifestyle that I would live. Procrastinating homesteaders across America often find themselves with a list of unsolved problems they've "saved for a rainy day," and for some, that "Raney day" has come.

The homesteaders we work with on our long-running show *Homestead Rescue* are complete strangers until we walk down the driveway and meet them on day one. However, just as their homesteads see progressive, significant changes day after day, the day-by-day transformation of the homesteaders' mindset and enthusiasm eclipses the improved structures and land.

I'm no Rhodes scholar, but I'm becoming somewhat of a "back roads" scholar. These less-traveled dusty back roads leave concrete and pavement behind and, more often than not, provide access to remote properties where you find farms, ranches, off-gridders, and twenty-first-century homesteaders.

I quickly realized that if I was going to significantly help these Lower 48 folks who have asked this northerner for help, I would need to adapt to the diverse landscapes, climates, subcultures, and economies that comprise our nation. And now, after five years on the road, we've helped over sixty homesteads in more than thirty different states, and I truly feel I can help anyone, with anything, anywhere.

URBAN RESCUE

A couple of years ago, I flew into LAX for a meeting with Discovery. Below me, the flats were filled with small, densely packed houses that stretched to the limits of my view, the hills dotted with mansions and gated communities already angling to keep regular folk at bay. The freeways were backed up with traffic, and the residential streets were narrowed

xii — HOMESTEAD SURVIVAL

to single lanes by double-parked cars and congested with drivers jockeying to get wherever they were going.

As I looked down, it occurred to me: What if Alaska's 7.2 earthquake had struck California (population thirty-nine million)? What if the epicenter was near LA (population four million)? Just like in Alaska, the power would go out, meaning no electricity: i.e., no streetlights, no traffic lights, no gas stations, no running water, no flushing toilets, no cooking, no refrigeration, no air-conditioning, and eventually no operative cell phones. All landlines would go down. What percentage of the four million people in LA are prepared for just *one* of these to fail? Perhaps some. What percentage of the four million people in LA are prepared for *all* of these to fail? Perhaps . . . zero.

I'm scheduled to fly to LA for another meeting in two weeks. What's changed since my last visit? When I look out the plane's window this time, I will see hundreds of ships carrying thousands of containers holding millions of tons of product anchored offshore, waiting their turn to be unloaded. The once well-stocked shelves of grocery and big-box stores are looking emptier than I've ever seen them. And, ironically, the stuff is here; it's just marooned a mile or so from port, waiting its turn. Sure, the supply-chain tangles will straighten themselves out this time, but what happens if the next "bump in the road" is something worse than COVID? Perhaps a cyberattack on the banking system or the grid. Or God forbid, in these uncertain times, a war.

It's not just us: There are grid-dependent cities, full of millions of people relying on those said shelves for daily sustenance and survival, all over the world. And when those shelves get bare, people from the UK, India, South Korea, and beyond will take a hard look at the world and their crowded lives, wondering if there's a way out. The point? The urban escape is global. Just as concerned parents in Tennessee worry about their families' future, so worry the parents around the globe, for the exact same reasons.

Is the urban escape a global problem? To the contrary. The urban escape is a global *solution*. And, speaking of London, the British band the Animals nailed it when they encouraged us to "get outta this place. . . . There's a better life for me and you."

I agree with Eric Burdon's sentiment. But, with inflation getting ever more extreme, you may be wondering if this is the time to make a big move. After all, 89 percent of the

The urban escape is global.

US stock market is owned by just 10 percent of the wealthy and, during the pandemic, that 10 percent watched their wealth grow by 45 percent.

Meanwhile, as the rich are getting richer, people have seen their food and daily-needs prices rise 35 percent, while gas prices have reached a seven-year high. Yet this demographic still plods along, working a lifetime of forty-plus-hour weeks, as the suburban American dream crumbles around them. And whether you realize it or not, these hardworking 90 percent are concerned about those empty shelves. They're hurting from that 35 percent inflation and record-high gas prices. Many are looking hard at the uncertain future of their surroundings and are scouring rural properties in search of something better.

So is it prudent to relocate in these financially uncertain times? The answer is a resounding, confident yes! In fact, I'm even recommending expediency in doing so. Many of us measure success against something other than the gold standard. Yet it's that quality-of-life standard, i.e., peace of mind, happiness, contentment, joy, independence, and a life of self-reliance, that really counts. These qualities are not for sale, but they are within the reach and affordability of any and all who recognize their value. And regardless of their backgrounds, the end goal is the same for all: a better quality of life.

So who are these homesteaders, and why are they compelled to make a big move? One couple had a daughter witness a drive-by shooting in Phoenix. That event motivated those parents toward their dream to live off-grid in beautiful, peaceful rural Arizona. Another family, from Reno, Nevada, lost their family home in the 2008 economic bust. They loaded up their vehicles and headed east to rural Lovelock, Nevada, where they bought forty acres for six thousand dollars. They are content and haven't looked back. Another couple near Seattle saw an increase in the crime rate and decided to move with their two sons to near Bonners Ferry, Idaho. Sometimes it's more husband than wife. Sometimes it's more wife than husband. But ultimately, couples and families are analyzing where they are on the road of life, and they don't like where they're heading. More than one homesteading couple just wanted to live peacefully and away from the madding crowds after serving multiple tours in the Middle East.

Another family lived for years at the edge of an airport. The dad told me he could read the lettering on the tires of the 747s as they dropped in for a landing over his head. He was desperate to improve his family's situation, but you don't live on the very edge of the airport if you can afford to live anywhere else. After enduring the noise for years, there was a breaking point, and they moved to rural Michigan, to a small plot of land deep in the woods and surrounded by quiet.

Millions have come to the crossroads, contemplating a drastic change—for better or for worse.

Listen. I've met and spent significant time with each of these families you've just read about (and many, many more), and I have personally asked them, "Was moving out here a good decision?" Unanimously they've all answered, unhesitatingly, "Yes."

Of course, many of the people we work with aren't running from violent neighborhoods, nor are they necessarily struggling with some aspect of their lives. I'd say *all* of them see rural life as a more fulfilling life: more land, more freedom, fresh air, clean water, clear skies, safer towns, room for a garden, room for a greenhouse, chickens, ducks, rabbits, goats, pigs, and horses. Room for their kids to run free, without constant surveillance and worry. Room to breathe. Room to live. A new beginning.

Those selling a house in town may get a good financial head start on buying a rural property. But if you don't have a nest egg, not to worry: Many rural or off-grid properties will not have an engineered well or septic system, making it harder to get bank financing to purchase them. That means the seller has to owner-finance and "carry the paper." They'll want a down payment and a reasonable monthly payment, but it's a good way to get started if you're strapped for cash on hand or have iffy credit (providing you can convince the seller of your good character and intentions, of course).

Pick the state, town, or outskirts that you can afford and accept that some of our most iconic rural spots—Jackson Hole, Telluride, even Girdwood, Alaska—are out of reach for most. These areas used to be the mecca for a rural, outdoor, mountain lifestyle. But the rich found out about these special places and exploited them with commercialism, driving the prices up and the people out (including, ironically, the army of waiters, valets, window washers, and other service people required to keep their log cabin mansions and lifestyles gleaming).

Not to worry. I've been everywhere, and *everywhere I've been has everything you're looking for.* The farther from town, the cheaper the land. Off-grid land will be less than on-grid. I prefer the mountains, and from the Appalachians to the Cascades (with the Rockies in between) there's millions of acres of mountain country awaiting. Like it hot? Arizona. Texas. Georgia. Alabama. Louisiana. Florida. Like it cold? There's numerous higher elevations that see plenty of snow and cold. You get it. The North American landscape is as diverse as

its potential settlers. There truly is something somewhere for everyone. Work in
harmony with your dream. Kick more
than one tire. Make crazy lowball offers
on properties. I shouldn't tell you this, but
a number of homesteaders bought their

Work in harmony with your dream.

land sight unseen. Remember the Robinsons in Tennessee (we built them a yurt in Season
Nine of *Homestead Rescue*)? Yep. They bought it without ever seeing it. Then they drove
across the country in a bus to the unseen property and months later stumbled across a well
they never knew they had (nor did the seller, apparently).

I don't recommend this process, but I'm learning that every property I've ever worked on
will eventually become a dream home to someone. However, some properties are more difficult than others (like ours). Due diligence and a visceral, up close and personal, "two feet on the
ground" tour of your prospective land is the best way to familiarize yourself with its pros and
cons. If you like the area, talk to people in town and you may stumble across properties not yet
on the market. I was running in training for a Denali expedition (I guided climbing expeditions
on the mountain starting in 1987), and about three days a week I'd pass by a cool property near
Hatcher Pass. Each time I'd think to myself, "I should stop and ask these people if this property
is for sale." So one day I jogged right up to a small cabin and did just that. The owner said, "We
are letting our friends buy it, but they haven't given us any money . . . yet." I wrote down my
number and said, "Call me if they don't come through with the down payment."

Two weeks later they called. Boom! I scrounged up the down payment, and over the last
ten years, I have built six rental cabins on this property (which is less than two miles from
our forty-acre homestead). Today, it's worth well over six hundred thousand dollars, but
none of this would have ever happened had I not taken the initiative (and broken a sweat or
two building the log cabin rentals).

I don't believe in luck, but I am a huge proponent of this adage: You'll never know unless
you try. Don't wait for a better economy, because it may not be coming. Take a calculated
risk and dare to fail. Go for a drive, look at properties, and know that those people are faring
better in these uncertain times than those in the city. You'll see their gardens. You'll see their
greenhouses. You'll see their barns, coops, and fences. And if you look hard enough, you may
see yourself looking into the rearview mirror, waving goodbye to your old life for . . . good.

ONE

THE HOMESTEADER MENTALITY

The desire to live freely, deliberately, and simply under the banner of homesteading is alive and well

As I travel from homestead to homestead, the plane's window becomes a wide lens into the past, focusing on the vast North American landscape below. And, at thirty-five thousand feet, I watch a historical documentary unfold in geographic increments: cities surrounded by suburbs, suburbs blended away to occasional rural villages, and then, there they are. The indelible survey section gridlines—now visible as roads or fence lines—carving out the homesteads and farmlands that can be traced to the Civil War–era Homestead Act of 1862, an act that allowed *any* American, whether rich or poor, to receive a 160-acre plot of land for a filing fee of eighteen dollars.

Abraham Lincoln believed that the role of government should be "to elevate the condition of men, to lift artificial burdens from all shoulders and to give everyone an unfettered start and a fair chance in the race of life." And for a period of time lasting well over a century, Americans were able to claim their lot in life. It wasn't a perfect system, and looking back we have to acknowledge the bad as well as the good: Although newly freed Black Americans were technically able to claim land this way, few successfully did. Indigenous tribes were forcibly removed from their homelands, causing generational despair and great loss of life. People abused the system too, with wealthy homesteaders figuring out ways to claim multiple homesteads in good locations. Lincoln's actions reshaped this country, and by the close of the act, over four million homestead claims were filed in more than thirty states, with the last being claimed by a man named Ken Deardorff, along the Stony River in Alaska in 1976.

Those dreamers carved a legacy of self-sufficient homesteads, farms, ranches, and orchards, all the way to the Pacific Ocean and then north to Alaska. From my window seat, I can easily see the fenced, bordered sections of land, each section representing 640 acres, or one square mile. The patchwork of squared farmland is a timeless reminder of where we came from, and where our food still comes from.

Two hundred years later, however, the migration has reversed, with young people going from the farm, to the factory, to the office. Many of the original "square mile" farms have been broken down to smaller tracts of 320, 160, 80, or 40 acres, and so on. The first subdivision was most likely built on an old homestead, since a two-acre homesite is worth five times more than a two-acre potato field.

The transition from family farms to factories was exacerbated as World War II came and went. Interestingly, the subdivisions we see everywhere were actually "invented" during that era—an amazing, novel idea at the time. The original two-, four-, six-, and eightplexes evolved into apartment and condominium housing en masse. Homesteads were surveyed, and developers greedily carved them into one-acre lots, and boom: We planted houses in the fields, resulting in the first fruits of shiny, sprawling suburbia. And, just like the rows of corn planted by the farmer as close together as possible to yield maximum profit, the concrete and wood bumper crop planted by developers has left us all living as close as we possibly can to each other—for the same reason: profit.

The overcrowding serves as a petri dish for pandemics, unrest, anxiety, and a culture lacking the fundamental core to keep it all together under a stressful, straining, burdensome load. As the original farms dissolved, so did the original homesteaders' legacy of knowledge and experience: Many of their descendants have forgotten the skill sets needed to thrive self-sufficiently. Today 330 million Americans are completely dependent on the grid, the grocery store, and the gas station to survive, day by day. Take one of those away from the city *or* the suburb, for just one day? Chaos. Panic. Twenty-four hours of disruption could put those crowded, grid-dependent masses in real danger.

SALT AND CABBAGE

That ancestral memory of homesteading is closer to the surface than you might realize. Think of sauerkraut: It's salt, cabbage, and a little physical labor. Take any root vegetable, immerse it in a brine, and leave it in your cellar or pantry; you are now a little more prepared for a food shortage than you were ten minutes ago. That combination of vegetable, mineral, and fermentation is so simple you don't need a recipe, so commonplace that every culture in the world practices some variation of it, and so essential to early homesteading that most early root cellars would have been lined with jars or crocks of it. The skills a successful homesteader needs are never more than a generation or two lost in the past. What is harder to recover is that spirit of homesteading, that willingness to take a chance and work collectively toward a difficult and labor-intensive goal. My family has succeeded at homesteading because we are willing to work hard *and* because we share a common vision of what a well-lived life looks like. So when you begin to consider a homesteading life, ask yourself, "What is our family vision? Do we have what it takes to stand together, united, come what may?"

PUTTING THE *HOME* INTO HOMESTEAD

Homesteading is a group activity. Successful homesteads have a cohesive, functioning family at their core.

A few years ago, I was buying three hundred feet of steel cable to build the tram to our homestead. I was going to trust my wife and kids to this cable on a daily basis, and a dunk from twenty feet into our freezing, rushing river might not be survivable in August, let alone December.

> Homesteading is a group activity.

I ended up buying good, quality cable. Now, 99 percent of all cable you'll ever see is comprised of six strands of wire rope wrapped around a single, straight strand called the core. Without its core, all of those strands become less productive. As pressure and stress are added to the cable's load, each strand relies on the core more to keep everything together, united, and strong. I looked at this six-strand cable as if it represented the six members of my family. And then I started thinking about *all* those families who homesteaded in North America.

As those farmers made the move from farm to factory and ultimately to the office over the last century, they left significant core values behind. In retrospect, each transitional step toward "progress" has found us working harder and harder for wages that are worth less and less. As commuters move farther away in search of affordable homes, commuting even longer distances becomes the norm. Suddenly that nine-to-five has essentially become a seven-to-eight. Now Mom and Dad are stressed to the max, the kids resent and exploit their absence, and that family unit, powered by love, respect, and faith, begins to crumble.

Once upon a time, the American dream seemed as strong as any cable: unbreakable. Every family member worked in harmony and carried their own load.

As my family worked together to install the tram and string the cable, I thought about how my six family members worked together like those six strands of wire. The "core" of our family success is and always has been an honest day's work and, at the end of an honest day's work, gathering to share our plans and talk about it over a plate of good food. Unfortunately, the simple rituals of the kitchen table, where a strong, working family unit gathered together willingly and regularly at least once a day for an entire lifetime, are all but gone.

I firmly believe that our cultural core is disintegrating. We are unraveling and becoming weaker as families, as communities, and as a country. At every juncture, be it the farm, the factory, or the office, we have left behind our values, our ethics, our skill sets, and our belief systems in the wake of chasing the elusive American dream.

If families aren't gathering at the traditional dining room table, where *are* they gathering? No matter how small or remote their hometown, it will have at least two of the two hundred thousand fast-food restaurants peppered across America. Fifty million Americans per day sit down at these restaurants. The food they eat is loaded with salt, preservatives, and bad fats. And once inside? Nine out of ten people will immediately find themselves engaged not with each other, but with an inanimate, lifeless electronic replacement for human interaction. We're all guilty, myself included.

I can't offer the American family the solution to the financial woes that might plague them. But I can offer another way of life, one that I feel is available to nearly all of us, if we are willing to take a chance on difficulty and discomfort: to be too hot, too cold, too wet, or too dry for the years it takes to get a homestead established.

The family unit and its core values that were brought to and taught at the kitchen table consistently, day after day, produced a formidable generation that built America's airplanes, cars, trucks, interstates, bridges, dams, and rails. And, at sixty-six thousand miles per hour (our current speedometer reading as we orbit the sun), we're getting further and further away from the farm, the garden, and the greenhouse. The skill sets needed to be self-sufficient feel lost. The independent spirit to be self-reliant seems to be forgotten. In these advanced modern times, when we rely on everyone and everything (except ourselves) to supply us with our every need (water, food, housing, power, sewers, heat, and air-conditioning), it's wise to ruminate on the increasing necessity of self-preservation. What would happen if the grid went down in a populated area such as Los Angeles, population four million, or New York City, population eight million? The impact could be catastrophic. Especially in winter . . .

We don't know what forces will shape our future: human error, cyberattack, earthquake, or something no one saw coming, like COVID-19. It's a changed and changing world. At this point in time, nothing would surprise me. But we have the option to prepare for it, to survive it, or, better yet, to avoid it completely.

TWO

HOW TO FUND YOUR HOMESTEAD

BUYING YOUR LAND

Just about anywhere I've gone in America you can buy land for 10 percent down, and people seem to be inclined to carry the note. If a house mortgage is out of your reach—and it is for many—buying vacant land, perhaps with a conventional mortgage, or more likely with owner financing, is achievable. If you have limited money and are willing to be miles from a town or even a paved road, you can get in for a few thousand down—*if* the owner is willing to strike a deal with you. This may require credit and employer references. However, one advantage of owner financing is that you can talk directly to the owner and negotiate with them outside of the structure of a traditional bank. Be direct, be honest, and don't play games or overpromise. Owner-financed generally means you will be paying off the loan much faster than you would with a traditional mortgage. Are you going to be able to make the payments? Be realistic, and don't commit yourself to a purchase you can't pull off.

Finally, make sure that the person claiming to be the owner is actually the owner, and that the title is free and clear and can be sold. IRS liens, for instance, can complicate a sale. Make sure that the deed reflects what you think you are buying. Never buy a piece of land until you've hired a title company to research the history of that property. We've worked with homesteaders who didn't own land they thought was theirs—not disastrous in their cases, but it could be hugely problematic and heartbreaking in others. Make sure you do your due diligence, and if you have any doubt about the legitimacy of the owner or the land, keep asking questions 'til you are sure of the answer. Research the different ways that an owner financing agreement can be structured, understand what happens if you default, and get a local real estate lawyer involved to go over the agreement before you sign. Some will not heed that advice, but all need to heed *this* advice: Never, ever buy a piece of land without a completed title search.

When you find a property that catches your eye, get the full and proper address, and go to the county or borough assessor's site to clarify that the property is zoned in a way that will allow both residential *and* agricultural use. The key thing is *agricultural*. If the property is strictly residential, you may not be able to live your homestead dream. Everything from chickens to goats might be problematic, and you may be in a constant battle with the county and possibly your neighbors to keep them.

Before you buy, understand what you're taking on, and make sure each and every member of your homesteading family is in agreement on the plan. Not that anything will go exactly according to that plan, but it's important to look at the bare ground and have the same—or very similar—vision for what is going to be built there. It may be you're running from a life that has crumbled due to forces outside of your control. If so, know that every sentence you will read here was written to help you get *back in control* of your new life, your new future, and your new beginning.

That few thousand dollars has given you the first page of a story that your family is going to be writing for the rest of your lives. All you need is the ability to see a vision, or the fulfillment of your dream, that first day you are standing on your own land. Things will happen slowly. It will take time. That's OK.

IMPROVING YOUR PROPERTY

Let's say you've bought your property. What next? Well, if it doesn't already have a living structure, you'll need to get to work. First: Take whatever money you're earning, and design and build your cabin. Small to begin with, and simple, just one room, maybe with basic electric and most likely no indoor plumbing. Jump ahead to the home section and build yourself a basic outhouse. Introduce animals when you can afford to shelter and feed them. You don't need power. You can haul your own water. You can live very basically. *It depends on how desperate you are to get started on a new life.*

Look around for farming grants: We have a nine-thousand-dollar grant pending right now, for building a barn to be used for farming, and if we spend ten thousand they'll reimburse us nine thousand for our barn. The Beginning Farmers and Ranchers loans page at usda.gov (usda.gov/topics/farming/grants-and-loans) has information about federal help. Your state may have its own programs (some states have grants for raising specific animals or growing specific crops). USDA grants are targeted and specific, but their standards are not—as of this writing—too onerous to meet. Your farm doesn't need to show a profit, and homesteading circles are full of tales of roadside vegetable or egg stands that allowed the homesteaders to meet the requirements for a loan. There are other specific loans for women or minority farmers, or farmers looking to set up some kind of supplemental business on their property. So your first stop on the internet should be the grant page at usda.gov. Tap into the homestead community in your area to see what other homesteaders are having success with.

Part of successful homesteading is committing to a shift in how you view yourself and your place in the world. If you can set aside those ideas about what success looks like, you have a real chance to build a meaningful, joyful, resilient life for yourself.

THREE

FIRST, FIND YOUR LAND

America has 2.26 billion acres with 330 million residents. Or so. And though I often say, "There's three kinds of people, those who can count, and those who can't . . ." even my math is good enough to tell me that's roughly seven acres per person, should we divvy it up evenly. The diverse, sweeping landscape defining North America has plenty to choose from when it comes to land. Hot. Cold. Dry. Wet. There's a piece of land for everyone. Literally. I recommend buying property that borders state or federal land. Our Alaskan property borders state land. Millions of undeveloped wilderness acres serve as our private hunting grounds, exclusive backcountry hiking trails, and a personal outdoor sanctuary. Thousands of these properties are available at low, affordable pricing. And depending on the state, permits for tree harvesting are made available to the public. The State of Alaska currently has such a program, and I have walked from our forty acres onto adjacent state land and harvested dead spruce trees, both as firewood and logs for the sawmill.

Alaska works for me. But it may not be perfect for you. So before you grab your checkbook, think carefully about what you need from the land, and whether the land will be able to sustain you. Put down that

There's a piece of land for everyone.

checkbook and step away from that outstretched hand ready to "shake on it." At the end of this chapter is a checklist, so get it out and assess the property carefully. That beautiful piece of land you're looking at has been doing just fine for millions of years, until you came along. Now you're asking it to sustain you, and you have needs. You'll need healthy soil and elevation to keep you out of floods' way. You'll want to be far, far away from pollution or contaminants. Water is key: The average on-grid family uses eighty to one hundred gallons of water per day, though my family is living proof that you can thrive just fine on half of that. However, when your plans include a garden, a greenhouse, and livestock, ample water is needed. You can live forty days without food, four minutes without air, and four days without water. If you wait 'til that thirsty fifth day on the homestead to concern yourself with your land's water potential, you're too late.

This may sound over the top, but I've learned the hard way, over and over again, that rushing into a land purchase is nearly always a bad idea. Instead I force myself to take my time, knowing that it's better to lose out on a good piece of property than to buy a bad one.

HATCHER PASS

Almost forty years ago I was looking for land to build a home on for my family near Hatcher Pass, Alaska. Hatcher Pass is an area of outstanding beauty, shaped over thousands of years by the Little Susitna River and the mountains that rise above it. The first time I saw it, I knew it was home. I soon realized there wasn't any land for sale—or at least not at prices I could afford. Eventually I realized that Alaska had a program to sell parcels of "borough lands" (similar to land owned by a county). I quickly found forty acres of borough land on the edge of state lands at Hatcher Pass. Perfect. I went down to the local borough building and announced my intention to buy it. They said, "Great, now here's your paperwork," and I took home a stack of documents to begin filling out.

A few days later, the borough contacted me and said they had changed their minds. Seems they realized the significant financial gain that this property could generate for their bank account if they put it out to bid. Since time began these bureaucrats had no interest in this land, zero. But suddenly *my* interest had sparked *theirs*. Soon rumors began circulating about a grandiose ski resort being developed at Hatcher Pass. My would-be homestead was suddenly as sought after as an empty lot on the Las Vegas strip.

The borough officials I had approached with a fairly straightforward land deal now saw an opportunity to make big money. So now I found myself in a bidding war with the money people in our little Alaskan fishbowl. Financially, and as fishbowls go, I've always been a bottom feeder. But now I was swimming in waters over my head, as lodge owners, developers, speculators, and greedy note buyers loftily whispered offers in the hundreds of thousands of dollars for this last piece of available land before you enter Hatcher Pass.

I reached out to a contractor I had worked for and to my longtime climbing partner. Bigger fish. They did their due diligence, crunched some numbers, and decided to form an LLC. The goal of Hatcher Pass LLC was to develop the land, building million-dollar homes adjacent to the projected ski resort. But I never shared with these two solid, honest businessmen what my goal was.

I simply wanted to live as close to these mountains as possible, nothing else, and this was the last piece of land in the valley that was this close to the mountains.

We agreed on a bid amount and submitted it. It was a dollar amount I couldn't do on my own, and I was certain the boisterous talkers would outbid us. Weeks later the contractor, who was integral in Hatcher Pass LLC, called me saying we got it.

That was twenty-five years ago. The alleged fifty-million-dollar ski resort headlines came and went. Seven years later, another ski resort builder fanned the flames and the forty acres once again became topical. But that ski resort speculator also came, saw, and went.

As the years passed I found myself remembering those early days, when I would wade the raging river just to walk on that forty acres, dreaming of building a log cabin for my family.

Finally, almost three decades after I first tried to buy the property, the day came. I approached each partner and expressed my true intentions for the forty. I offered to buy them out. As businessmen, they cautiously said, "No."

I told them I never was interested in the money or the development. I just wanted to "live like an Alaskan should live." Within a few months' time, each allowed me to buy them out, at their full asking price, and twenty-five years later, my dream of living as close as one possibly can to Hatcher Pass and the mountains came true.

It was still exactly the same as the first day I set foot on it. Pristine. No bridge. No million-dollar homes. Only moose tracks and game trails weaving through brilliantly pink fields of Alaskan fireweed. Home.

It took me decades to buy the forty acres that Mollee and I now call home. If we could wait that long, then trust me, you can wait the time it takes to read this chapter, and run through the checklist at the end of it.

WHICH STATE IS FOR YOU?

I always knew that Alaska was home, at least for me. And a lot of homesteaders find themselves looking at a map of the Lower 48 and wondering just where *their* home might be. There are pros and cons to just about every rural area in the country, and the best way to sift through all the possibilities is to understand your own priorities. What are your goals and hopes for your homestead? Is homeschooling your kids a priority? Or raising a certain kind of meat animal, or growing a specific crop? Are you looking for climate resilience (in which case, pick the disaster you feel most able to survive, and buy accordingly)? Once you understand what you want, it will be easier to find a place that fits you and your family's needs.

All fifty states allow homesteading, but some have more restrictions than others. New York has some restrictions on off-grid living. Tennessee actively welcomes homesteaders. Some states have laws protecting a primary residence in the event of bankruptcy. Idaho, home to over sixty thousand homesteads, is very welcoming to homesteaders, with laws that protect homesteaders' rights to homeschool children, raise livestock, and grow crops. Ohio is also friendly to homesteaders, with many counties having relatively lenient building codes. And Alaska has minimal laws and regulations to get in the way of your dreams. Missouri makes homesteading simple, and I think we've shot more episodes there than in any other state. Rainwater collection, for instance, is unregulated, and the local government is relatively hands-off on homesteaders, allowing them to live their lives as they see fit. Generally, states like Tennessee, Idaho, Oregon, Michigan, and Missouri are actively supportive of and welcoming to homesteaders—which explains the large numbers of homesteaders in all of these places. Temperate states like Florida and Hawaii make for an easier homesteading experience, since harsh winters aren't a factor. Northern Arizona is another good choice, except for a big problem we'll discuss in the next chapter (hint: water).

Numerous states offer free land to settlers willing to move to remote areas to help repopulate struggling communities. These offers change as homesteaders move in and take advantage of the opportunity, but most of these types of properties are located in the Great Plains. Right now, a homesteader willing to work hard could get a free lot in towns like Curtis, Nebraska, or Lincoln, Kansas, to name a few. Some of these opportunities come with stipulations like building a certain amount of structures within a year. Still, free land is free land! If at least one member of your family can earn a living working remotely, this could be an excellent option for you.

As you're researching, factor in whether you are planning to go fully off the grid. Living off the grid is legal in all states (with various rules and regulations). However, even if you build your cabin yourself with recycled or upcycled materials, you will still be liable for property taxes on it. You will still have to follow local building codes and local zoning restrictions. Many areas have minimum home sizes, so keep that in mind if you want to go the tiny-house route. Some ban long-term camping on your property, even as you build your home.

Finally: No matter how tempting it might seem, don't even think about squatting on seemingly abandoned property. Every square inch of land in this country belongs to someone or something. And eventually that person or group will notice their "abandoned" farm has some new residents. No matter how you spin it, no one is going to thank you for your labors. There's an old cowboy saying that goes like this: "Don't squat with your spurs on." And I might add, when it comes to this topic, "Don't squat . . . anywhere."

GROW ZONES

As you look at the fifty options available to you, one of your biggest considerations should be how exactly you are planning to feed your family and move toward self-sufficiency. For most homesteaders a garden is a big part of their plans, so take a few minutes to understand how the average yearly temperature range will affect your plans.

There are eleven different planting zones (or growing zones) in the US. Zone 1 and Zone 2 dominate much of Alaska, although our Aleutian Island chain and Panhandle in particular have some other growing zones. In the Lower 48, only the northernmost reaches of some states (along the Canadian border) fall in Zone 3. Zones 4 to 8 form lateral bands across many of the states. And the Hawaiian Islands are home to several of the more tropical grow zones. These numbers can give you some useful information about temperature and what plants will thrive, and when. You can enter a zip code at planthardiness.ars.usda.gov to get detailed information about the specific temperature ranges of any property in the United States.

Here's the thing: You can homestead in any of these zones. Some are easier than others, or more suited for year-round growing. Some, like our home in Hatcher Pass, require greenhouses and optimal sunlight to grow, even in summer. But you can grow enough food to feed a family pretty much anywhere in this country. Successful growing is less about zones and location than it is about the four essentials: sun, site, soil, and hard, hard work. We'll talk more about this in the gardening chapter, but for now, understand that so long as your location has good soil, good sun, and preferably a south-facing exposure, and so long as you are willing to do the hard graft to go from seeds to greens, you will be able to grow there. Caveat: Make sure you do your research as outlined in the water and gardening chapters before you buy. You can grow anywhere *except* land that has polluted soil or water.

NARROWING DOWN THE SEARCH

By now you hopefully have some idea of where in this country you want to make a home. But if you don't, consider these factors too. In the end, the perfect homestead for you is the one that meets the majority of your needs—*and* the needs of your family. I can't overstate how crucial it is that a homestead is not simply one person's dream. Your homestead experience will be cut short if not all family members are on board. In a few pages there is a more detailed checklist for assessing a specific property. However, as you look for the general location you want to settle in, consider:

Natural Resources: We will cover this in later chapters, but good water, healthy soil, and ample sunlight are essential.

Local Community: Even if your goal is to live an isolated life, there are going to be times you will need and want good neighbors. This is doubly true if one member of the homestead is less inclined to solitude than another. So find a property that has some kind of community within a few hours' drive. And remember that even if you can find an isolated spot, you're never going to be *in isolation*. Your land and your homestead exist in relation to all the other homesteads and townships around you, so look at it holistically, and don't fall in love with a property that is surrounded by people or places that are objectionable to you.

Cost of Living: The homesteading dream is to live completely self-sufficiently, but realistically you are going to be buying gas, hardware items, food, and even water until your homestead is up and running.

Regulations, Property Codes, and Taxes: We've had multiple moments on *Homestead Rescue* when a plan was foiled at the last minute by an obscure building code or municipal regulation. Make sure you've done all of your research before you buy. Will your local municipality insist on a septic system or be OK with a composting toilet? What are the requirements for housing structures? If you are planning something unconventional, make sure your plan meets building codes before you even begin. There's no worse feeling than having a shipping-container home and nowhere to put it.

THE VERY BEST PLACE TO HOMESTEAD IS . . .

The number one question I get from would-be homesteaders is "Where should I buy?" As you're probably realizing, there is no one answer to this question. And *my answer*, "Alaska," is most likely the wrong answer for you. So the best place to homestead is the place that gives you the greatest chance to succeed, and establish a homestead that will survive and thrive for decades. The number one indicator of a homestead's chances of success isn't a "perfect property" or an ideal location. Instead, the best sign that a homestead will flourish is a homestead family that is joined together by a common vision and dream.

The truth is there is no perfect place, anywhere. Whatever land you will buy will have flaws and problems. The good news is that your land can always be improved, and in most cases a "bad plot" can be made better with some hard work and ingenuity. I've met and worked with hundreds of people who thought they had bought their dream piece of land—only to have that dream turn into a nightmare. A few years ago we worked with a couple who bought a beautiful piece of land, with a seemingly well-made cabin, on a hill in Wisconsin. Everything looked great, at least at first glance. The hill was covered in lush vegetation. No wonder they had fallen in love with it. The romance lasted until the first big summer storm, when a county culvert, above their property line, flooded their property—over and over again. We looked under the foundation and saw that the corner support beams were on the verge of failing. *Not good.*

This was a couple who had scraped together every penny to invest in this property. There was no backup plan for their unstable house and top-soil-free garden. Here's where homesteaders are different, and where that homestead mentality comes into play. By pulling together and working hard, we were able to save the dwelling structure, salvage their dream, and begin the process of refortifying their soils. I've never met a homesteading family where we were unable to improve their property—or at least improve their odds of being able to grow and live on it. The best option when you are looking for land is to *buy good land*. The second-best option is to invest time and effort into improving what you have or can afford.

THAT GUY

Once you've narrowed down where you think you want to establish your homestead, now comes the hard work. The first thing on your checklist is simply this: Talk to the next-door neighbor. Who knows that general region, and that piece of land, better than him? Certainly not me. Definitely not a real estate agent. And beware of the seller who may "know all," but chooses not to reveal all.

The neighbor will have a history of working the property's soil. He or she knows what grows well and what doesn't. He or she will most likely also know the well depths throughout the region. Look at nearby homesites. Flourishing gardens? Burgeoning greenhouses? If so, your due diligence is paying off big time. Lush vegetation means adequate water and good soil. If the wells are three hundred to five hundred feet deep, find out the price per foot. Some places charge fifty dollars per foot, and it adds up fast. The average cost of an American water well ranges from four to fifteen thousand dollars. So ask "that guy" who drilled their well. If they don't know, ask around, find the local well driller, and give them a call. Well drillers are worth their weight in . . . water, and for the most part will give you the straight scoop with their experiences drilling on surrounding properties. Disappointed property owners aren't great for their business, and if they think you are unlikely to find water, they will tell you.

Does the property have good south-facing slopes? Are the lowlands susceptible to flooding? If it is in a floodplain you'll be hard-pressed to get a home insured. Many properties have springs, ranging from a veritable trickle to a small stream flowing directly out of the side of the hill. Most likely that water will be fine once developed, but does that spring run year-round? Many creeks (especially in the west) are seasonal, or controlled by dams or other water infrastructure upstream. Be mindful of the fact that you might be looking at the property on its very best day (especially relevant and likely if a real estate agent is showing it to you). What types of issues may potentially surface on this property?

While walking around any property you can empty your store-bought plastic water bottle, fill it with the water from the property, and have it tested. You'll have basic test results within a week. As you tour your potential homestead property, look for bedrock, clay, wet areas, and gravel. Remember, you have a driveway, a house pad, and a septic system to put in. If water is life, then gravel is gold—having it on the property may save you thousands in building materials. Is the property waterfront? Lake? River? This type of property commands a higher price tag but obviously is worth it if you can afford it.

Your final assessment will be a mix of all these different factors—this will help you to determine which property is optimal for you. Prioritize and decide if the potential problems are within your ability to deal with. Homesteading comes with risk, and you and your family have to be OK with the possibility of danger or destruction in order to begin this adventure. Remember, short of an utter catastrophe, most homesteads can be saved, salvaged, and restarted. And, for resilient homesteaders, a catastrophe doesn't have to be the end of the story, as one family in Hawaii found out.

WHEN THE LAND YOU LOVE DOESN'T LOVE YOU BACK

A few years ago I was called to Hawaii to help a young couple, new parents of a baby girl, who'd lost their new homestead to a lava flow. The couple had purchased five acres, built a beautiful home, and spent every cent they had while doing so. Soon after their homestead completion, BOOM! Kīlauea erupted, releasing a massive river of molten lava, spewing and spouting at 2,000 degrees Fahrenheit, roaring down the mountainside to the ocean's shore, dissolving, burning, and entombing everything in its destructive path, including everything the couple owned. Walking around on the lava field I asked, "Where is your home?" Their answer? "Thirty feet down, right where you're standing." It was hard to believe, and even harder to comprehend. I remember thinking to myself, "Why rebuild here? How?" But after listening to the young (basically homeless) couple, it was apparent that this now five-acre lava flow was still their homestead.

The husband started pointing out what remained of their life: a few small patches of green on the edge of the flow. Their battered pickup. Even as he talked I kept coming back to the fact that everything they owned, from shovels and hoes, to family albums, to pots and pans, was buried under a layer of *lava* so thick it wouldn't fully erode for millions of years. Eventually the forest would reclaim the land, but for now no trees meant no shade, doubly problematic as the tropical sun radiated off of the black rock. Their once-fertile soil and burgeoning garden were black and gray, devoid of life. And it had buried everything they owned. So formidable was this palette that I was apprehensive of our first brushstroke.

I felt these kids' pain. Picking the right tract of land is the very first, and arguably the most important, choice a homesteader can make. Good land anywhere is expensive. Good land in Hawaii is doubly so (not helped by billionaires scooping up vast ranches of ancestral and indigenous lands in Kauai, or entire islands, like Lanai). Affordable land is affordable for a reason: The Ocean View Estates subdivision in the Hawaiian islands has 10,500 one-acre lots, perhaps the largest subdivision in America.

Every single one of these properties lies within the potential path of lava flow.

Lava.

Flow.

I understood the risk these two kids had taken, but at that moment they felt like they had made the biggest mistake of their lives. They had sunk everything they owned into a piece of property that had almost killed them. Their big plans of creating a home and business that they could pass on to their daughter had evaporated along with all of their money, energy, and hope. I knew that if we didn't do something fast they would feel like their only option was to go home to the mainland—something they emphatically didn't want to do.

Those kids had done something I've done a million times myself: made a mistake. As someone who has lived in the harshest environment in the fifty states for nearly fifty years, I have no hesitation telling people that I have probably made far more mistakes than they ever will. In that same breath I think it also qualifies me to help other people avoid them.

———————————

As we walked across the rough and razor-sharp A'a' lava (supposedly named because of the sound you make when you step on it with bare feet), I began to see why they had fallen in love with their land: The edges of the jungle were rich and lush, ready to grow coconuts, cacao, and citrus. In the distance we could see the ocean, and an on-shore breeze was beginning to cool the property.

And then . . . while walking around a rugged jumble of jagged lava rubble, I saw it. Hope. A small, brilliantly green plant growing out of a sea of predominantly blackish lava rock that stretched out for miles and disappeared into the Pacific Ocean. In less than one year's time, and as a cooling lava flow still emitted ten thousand small steaming geysers, life found a way to start the revegetation process . . . naturally. That one chunk of volcanic rock picked up enough organics to sprout a plant. One can easily see that with just the slightest soil, these balmy islands will supply ample sun and rain to grow anything you want.

Every piece of land has its potential risks, and for homesteaders, especially young ones like this couple, accepting risk might be the only way to be able to afford that dream land. I've done it myself: My new house is built on a fault line, separated from the road by a white-water river, and built on the edge of a two-hundred-foot cliff. Homesteading is risky. And your biggest risk comes with your biggest purchase: acreage.

WORKING WITH WHAT YOU HAVE

Hawaii is a tricky place to get permits, especially when you are in a hurry. At the same time we were dealing with the Hawaii conundrum: If we built a permanent structure—even if we could get a permit—they were still living with a good chance of being destroyed by *another* lava flow. The solution was of course a mobile home, ideally something drivable. They could live on the five acres and if the volcano erupted, they could drive out. We ended up buying two old buses, one that ran and one with a blown-out engine, taking the roof off of the smaller bus, building a small 8' by 10' loft, and creating a small living space that gave them—for the first time—ocean views. The bigger bus—which still ran—became the kitchen and living area.

First, however, we had to prepare the land. One option was the old-fashioned way: Let plants seed the land and slowly break it down with their roots. Alas, our family didn't have multiple thousands of years to spend waiting for this to happen. Instead, we spoke to a few locals, who helped us understand the difference between lava you can work with, and lava you can't.

When you move onto lava rock you get one of two types: The fresh lava rock crumbles and is not hard as a diamond. You can walk an excavator or 'dozer out there and use the weight of the machine to build a road and crush the lava down to flatten it out. By doing this, you can make sense of a lava flow fairly quickly. And in fact, in one day we were able to take a portion of the couple's property from a rough moonscape, riddled with gray jagged porous rocks and boulders, to resembling something you can build on.

This new "soil" is incredibly rich in minerals because it comes from the center of the earth. Even though it's not ideal, it *is* a starting point. And this gets back to the fascinating design of how volcanoes have shaped this planet: Look at Vesuvius, Krakatoa, and the Hawaiian islands. Their lava flows have transformed from something devoid of life to something that is teeming with life. Anything you introduce to those islands will be overgrown by thick and aggressive grasses (often the invasive guinea grass that crowds out native species and can be a significant problem on a homestead). It will become a jungle, and you'll need a machete to walk through it.

Once you've flattened the lava, you can accomplish a lot. The crushed lava is still porous (think of pumice rock, floating). If you were just to buy and lay down topsoil, the hellacious rains would quickly wash away your investment, leaching significant amounts of it down through the crushed lava. Nothing is cheap on those islands, so all that investment, all that planning—the money you've spent on soil and plants—would be gone too. What do you do? Fight lava with lava! In this case something called cinder. Unlike the black A'a' lava, cinder is red (if you've ever been to Hawaii you might have noticed the red soil in places like the hills of Kauai—this is cinder).

So after we crunched down the razor-sharp A'a' lava, we brought in cinder on a dump truck to top off the driveway. If we were building in a conventional place we'd have smoothed out the grade and used gravel or some other product to make the driveway smooth and walkable, or so your kid could ride a bike on it without killing themselves. And they have all those products on the islands of course, but homesteading is all about using what the natural world has to offer us. Cinder is cheaper, more readily available, and frankly more attractive than gravel (expensive) or asphalt (a no-go because it's nonporous—read more about it in the flash flood chapter). This cinder puts a cap on all of the millions of tiny voids in the black lava that have been crushed and trampled down, turning the lava into malleable pieces that you can flatten and smooth out.

After we laid down the cinder, that porous lava rock was essentially sealed off. Now the couple could bring in topsoil and start planting. First, trees: mangos, avocados, bananas, coconuts, and cacaos. These trees grow fast, sending roots out that will further break down the black lava. In ten years these trees will be forty feet tall and teeming with fruit.

Two years from now that plantation will be full of tropical tree fruit, and a garden will be full of greens, gourds, tomatoes, and melons. The young couple's life will still be full of challenges and difficulties—as are all our lives. But this is part of the paradox of land: No matter where you buy, or what you do, there will be moments where the land seems to be actively trying to repel you. Lava is this couple's challenge, but on other parts of the islands we've worked with homesteaders dealing with flash floods, toxic slugs, feral pigs, or invasive grasses that just won't quit. All of these Hawaii homesteaders are facing their individual challenges and adapting to them, in often ingenious ways. The pigs aren't going away; neither are the slugs. The volcano? Not going anywhere! Some of these couples may have to run from floods, molten lava, or fire in the future. But they, like all homesteaders, are making the most of what Mother Nature has to offer. And even if they do have to run, I'm sure they will return, once again, to rebuild and continue their homesteading dream.

MAKING SENSE OF THE LAND

Here's what I learned from that couple in Hawaii, and what every homesteader needs to know as they look over a piece of land that has thrown a curveball at them: Don't stand there dumbfounded and overwhelmed. Take action. Make sense of it. One step at a time.

I've guided climbing expeditions on Denali, the highest mountain in North America, multiple times. It's a demanding climb, and sometimes we don't reach the top. Each time I approached the mountain the same way: one step at a time. It's not my steps that change from year to year, but things outside of my control. Usually it is the weather turning bad, generally near the top. The climb gets steeper, there is less oxygen, and it gets more dangerous. Perhaps you cut a corner, and didn't factor in enough food or fuel to outlast a storm or two, and it backfired. Now you are out of fuel, and you have to think about the lives that you, as a guide, have brought into this harsh environment. You turn around and begin your descent. Failure.

Take action. Make sense of it. One step at a time.

Likewise you, as the homesteader, need to keep going step by step, constantly evaluating and making sense of the land. A successful homesteader approaches his or her land in a practical, pragmatic, logical, and deliberate way: From every tree you cut down to every shovel of dirt you turn over. By being deliberate and thoughtful you have the best chance to take full advantage of your land's potential. Before you buy, you will assess your soil for growing, assess your trees for timber, and pick the sunniest location for passive heat for your home and garden. If you fail to do this then you haven't made sense of your land; in fact, you've unwittingly shown a disrespect for the land.

I'd go so far as to say there is no bad land, but there are homesteaders who don't take the time to understand their land. Understand that the "lay of your land" will make you change your plans, and the more willing you are to adapt to the physical reality of your surroundings, the better your chances of success.

YOUR LAND PURCHASE CHECKLIST

1. **Water.** We'll talk more about this in the next chapter, but a reliable, clean water supply is essential. Sure, you can truck water in, or rely on catchment. But realistically these strategies are going to wear you down and temper the joy and happiness you take in homesteading. (Catchment is passive, but in most cases I wouldn't rely on it for drinking water without filtration and ozone treatment.) So pick a property with a clean, safe, reliable water source and exercise due diligence to ensure you have rights to that water.

2. **Location.** You need to consider two things here. One is big picture. Are you moving to rural Florida or to the Montana mountains? Two is finding the right location within that general area. These are big decisions, so pick carefully. A good rule of thumb is that you want a property with a generous, south-facing area for your garden, unobstructed by trees or other obstacles that might block the sun. Morning sun is ideal; afternoon sun can overheat or dry out plants. So consider that too.

3. **Neighbors.** Do you want them? Remember that your feelings about neighbors may change as you get older. It's possible that having a friendly face close at hand will be valuable in the future even if you don't want them around now. Conversely, where you go, so will other humans. If peace and quiet are nonnegotiable for you, pick land that allows you to keep your homestead buildings and gardens out of sight from the road. As we have learned over the years, an attractive homestead will draw other homesteaders and conventional home builders into the neighborhood. Be aware too that new neighbors who value their privacy will not be the most welcoming folks if they feel you are invading their solitude. Build with this in mind, avoiding a conflict if you can by situating your structures away from shared property lines or existing homes and buildings.

4. **Existing buildings.** A homestead with a livable structure will require less initial time to establish, though you will also be dealing with a house that may or may not have been well maintained by previous owners. Keep your eye open for derelict buildings. Even if those barns or other structures are no longer safe or usable, they can be salvaged and scrapped and repurposed—potentially saving you thousands of dollars in materials and a lot of time given current lumber shortages. In Tennessee, I saw dozens of unused old barns worth substantial amounts of money if they were taken apart and repurposed. Caveat: They can be dangerous to break down, so dismantler beware.

5. **Existing infrastructure.** Are you going to need to put in a road, or will you be able to use a county or borough road to access your property? Gravel is the cheapest and longest-lasting option (and has some positive side effects, such as being permeable to water). Whatever route you take, don't forget to factor in the cost of a road or driveway into your budget.

6. **Zoning.** Make sure you research what kind of animals (and how many of them) you'll be able to keep. Ditto on your home build. Are there state, borough, or county requirements that are going to price you out, or require you to build a bigger home than you are planning?

7. **How much land?** Don't bite off more than you can chew. Two and a half to three acres is enough to keep chickens, a few meat animals, an extensive garden, and a greenhouse, as well as space for living structures and barns. Unused land is still going to require your attention: You'll want to keep invasive species like honeysuckle under control, and if you are in a fire-prone area you'll need to monitor and clear areas of land that become a fire hazard.

8. **Prior owners.** Make sure you explore all areas of your property for items previous owners may have left behind. Junk needs to be sorted, neatly organized into "reusable" piles, or cleared. This is especially important if you have children, as you don't want them getting injured by abandoned vehicles or old structures.

9. **Too good to be true.** Don't forget: *buyer beware*. If land feels too good to be true, you need to find out why. The skyrocketing prices of land and homes means that the true, quality bargains are few and far between. Ask yourself why no one has snapped up the acreage you are looking at. We've worked with homesteaders who bought land unaware that it was poisoned by mining effluent. Another family bought an idyllic-seeming farm, without realizing that the topography around them funneled relentless wind through their property. Ask the neighbors questions. Go into town, ask *more* questions. Keep asking, and don't stop until you have a good sense of the potential pitfalls of the land you are considering.

10. **Find a legitimate title company and have them execute a title search.**

FOUR

DRINKING WATER

Alaska has three million lakes and twelve thousand rivers. One of those rivers, the Little Susitna, separates me from the road system, civilization, and the grid. It's often a Class IV river when the big mountains shed their melting snow down countless valley drainages that collide into one cascading river torrent, making its way to the ocean over granite boulders the size of double-door refrigerators.

I fell in love with the majesty of Hatcher Pass and the Little Susitna as far back as the 1970s, and have been hiking, climbing, and skiing in those Talkeetna Mountains ever since. I've seen brown bears, black bears, moose, wolverines, Dall sheep, wolves, coyotes, fox, lynx, beavers, porcupines, marmots, and a longer list of birdlife. And they all live upstream from our homestead, bringing to mind the old saying, "Don't drink downstream from the herd." We have a beautiful small stream that flows through the middle of our forty-acre homestead. But I don't use that source for our water. Why? Because those herds come with friends: coliform bacteria. While not all coliform bacteria are problematic or harmful, some—including E. coli—are. So when you are scouting out your homestead it's important to know the difference between water and drinking water. There are other potential contaminants to think about as well—pollution and heavy metals, among others.

Finally, there is the biggest water problem of all: no water. In the summer of 2021 I was in Idaho. Now, potatoes are to Idaho as sasquatch is to Oregon, and both need water to survive. One acre can yield between thirty and sixty thousand pounds of potatoes. Yet when I went to help out a pair of homesteaders in Idaho, I found them on a sprawling eighty-three acres, "potatoless." Hmm. Why? No water, and steep mountainous terrain with hard granite lurking just beneath the skim coat of unassuming green grass.

We arrived during a drought, and temperatures were reaching 108 degrees Fahrenheit. The unprecedented "heat dome" was burning towns in Canada and evaporating lakes in California. Still, this young couple had a seemingly great setup: They had built a thirty-foot-diameter geodesic dome perched on a granite promontory, looking out over a lush, green, fertile valley with a large river flowing through it. A million-dollar view, literally.

Idaho was seeing a huge increase in people due to masses fleeing the cities seeking something less congested, or perhaps, less stressful. I talked with at least a dozen couples, mostly from California and Texas, who were scouring rural Idaho in search of a better life. That vision of free-flowing water, and wide-open spaces, was a big part of the draw. Yet many of these newcomers didn't understand the complex history of water in the west, or what they needed to contemplate before they bought their land. Interestingly, the Idaho homesteading couple we were helping were actually indigenous, and the wife was carrying on as a third-generation Idahoan homesteader following in the same steps as her mother and grandmother. Her husband kept referring to her as "the dreamer of the family," and as I worked alongside both of them I realized why. She had a strong connection with this heavily treed, steep, and rugged landscape. It was apparent she wanted to thrive, growing her own food and progressing the homestead legacy. But, as Bigfoot can tell you, it's hard to exist without water—and someone who believes in you.

Her husband definitely believed in her and willingly followed her dream. When I suggested I might be able to scratch out a flat area creating usable space, she was hopeful to put in a garden. He was hopeful to have a parking spot for his F350 flatbed. To each his/her own.

This couple—and dozens of other families and couples we've worked with over the last few years—were grappling with one of the biggest challenges any homestead will deal with: water, and specifically, either too much (flooding) or too little of it. We'll leave the "too much" for the next chapter, but for now, our water woes are of the strictly potable nature.

DRINKING WATER AND YOUR HOMESTEAD

Living in Alaska, "downstream from the herd" means moose and caribou. In the Lower 48, that "herd" includes commercially farmed animals as well. If you're homesteading in an area with agricultural operations, you need to dig a little deeper to see how these companies are—or are not—affecting the local water sources. But as with any location: talk, read, and listen before you make your purchase.

Farming communities sometimes have dangerously high levels of nitrates that seep into the water from manure or fertilizer. In coal country, heavy metals such as arsenic, lead, and copper can seep into aquifers, streams, and bodies of water. Not something you'd want to wash your clothes in, let alone drink. Fracking chemicals have been found in groundwater from Pennsylvania to Wyoming. If you're looking to settle in the west, you need to understand how the complex system of water rights may or may not affect your land. And finally, it's smart to cast an eye upward and understand the natural weather and climate systems of your potential new home. How they are changing and how they will continue to change are key to how successful your homestead will be long term.

None of these water issues needs to derail your plans, but understanding them will help you identify properties that are good choices, and properties that aren't. A gallon of water weighs 8.34 pounds. A family of four living conventionally uses twelve thousand gallons a month. Most homesteaders use far less, but even a fraction of that water weighs—literally—tons. I've met valiant homesteaders making daily water runs with ATVs and pickups, but a better plan is to ensure a reliable and safe water supply on your property before you buy.

BEFORE YOU BUY

THE SALTWATER WELL

"There's a sucker born every minute!" Truth be told, I've been that sucker more times than I want to admit. I've always wanted to trust people and believe that what they are telling (or selling) me is on the up and up. Many times they weren't telling me the *whole* truth, and somewhere in that process they got the gold mine and I got the shaft. Of all the tough questions you need to ask before you buy, tough questions about water are the most important. Don't buy a property unless you are completely certain that either there is adequate drinking water on the property, or you have a workable plan for trucking in water. I've heard a lot of heartbreaking stories about badly chosen properties over the years, but none hurt more than homesteaders who bought land with water that turned out to be the *wrong kind of water*. This came home for me one summer in Oregon, where I met a hardworking, honest young couple who had trusted the wrong real estate agent.

It was love at first sight for the prospective homeowners: nice home, outbuildings, privacy, and acres of land. They walked the property with the hard-selling real estate agent, toured the house, turned on the water, but never tasted it. Why? They'd been told it was good, and they didn't think to doubt the agent.

After scraping and scrounging every penny, they walked into their new home overwhelmed with first-time homeowner excitement (the purchase price was over two hundred thousand dollars). And then the wife decided to draw a glass of water, instantly spitting it back into the sink. The husband took a sip. Salt water. They tested all the taps in the house and found heavy salt throughout. They started to make some phone calls, but weeks went by without any results. They hired attorneys, but this was an added expense (and stress) that ultimately led to them accepting defeat. By now they'd learned that this part of Oregon did indeed have an issue with salt water found in water wells sporadically.

Their neighbors who bordered their property (left and right) had good wells free from salt, so they started saving to drill a new well. They called a well driller who went down seven hundred feet. Fifteen thousand dollars later, the first glass of water from that freshly drilled well had salt, and lots of it. Their homesteading dream of growing food, introducing livestock, and being self-reliant was all on the brink of dying of thirst.

The property was approximately seventy years old, making me wonder what the original homesteader did for water. Turns out there was about one foot of what looked to be a concrete culvert sticking vertically out of the ground with a concrete lid and barrel covering it. "What's that, guys?" They tell me it's most likely a well hand-dug by the original homeowner. "Have you ever opened it?" They hadn't. We cleared the barrel and debris from the lid and twenty feet down I could see and hear some water trickling in. It was tight, but big enough in diameter for me to drop down a ladder and climb in to investigate. There was about twenty gallons of water in the bottom, with water seeping in through holes in the culvert. It wasn't a lot, but it was hope. I drilled holes through the concrete (with a concrete drill and masonry bits) at the seep spots, thinking they would allow more water catchment from the sporadic rains. We slid the heavy concrete lid back over the top and walked away, giving it time to fill up. Perhaps.

Meanwhile, I noticed an adjacent property had a pond hidden in the forest. After nosing around a bit I deduced this particular part of Oregon has clay, and when you're having water problems, a little clay can change your day. Their homestead most likely had clay too, and even better, their terrain had the perfect slope to catch and "carry" water down to a clay-bottomed, water-holding pond. A big sloping hill to the left of the house would catch thousands of gallons of rainwater in short order. This area of Oregon is arid, so we also started putting gutters on their house, piping rainwater into catchment/storage tanks. Of course, firing up a huge excavator, clearing beloved trees (as all trees are), and digging a massive hole in the ground is quite invasive. I had to sell them on the plan even as I had to admit that if we didn't find ample clay this huge plan and "huger" mess were for naught.

They agreed and I began to dig. They watched the excavator pull bucket after bucket of black, rich dirt out of the ground. Normally, that's something to get excited about and we did, a little, but then we all were quickly reminded that gardens and greenhouses don't do too well, on any homestead, without water. Each bucketful of dirt yielded more and more dirt with no clay. Misty saw the potential of that soil and started moving it with a skid steer to a new garden site. No pressure!

And then, about six feet deep, there it was: clay. A much-needed ray of hope shot across that homestead. I throttled up the massive excavator and started moving hundreds of yards of earth. A few days later they had a significant pond complete with landscaping and built-in overflow. Still, it was the dry season, and I needed to know now if this huge hole (and my plan to help them) were both going to hold water. We organized a water truck to deliver water, ten thousand gallons in total. He backed it up to the pond's edge and opened the valve. I drove a stake in the ground at the high-water edge. Come morning that stake would tell me if the water was static, or receding out through the bottom. The next day it hadn't lost a drop; unbelievable.

The key to making a pond is to find a clay layer, spread it around thickly on every inch of the (hoped-for) pond surface, and then compact it with the tracks of an excavator or dozer, simply "walking the machine" back and forth across the bottom and up the side walls. If you live anywhere on Planet Earth and have an abundance of clay, you easily can have a pond. It naturally will fill to the brim with rains or snowmelt, and believe it or not, in most places that thing will stay full year-round. If you don't have indigenous clay, you can truck it in from elsewhere. I've done that before too. But there's no margin for error. You've heard, "Life finds a way." In this case, the question is "Does water find a way?" You bet Jurassic will.

DO YOUR RESEARCH

So don't be too quick to assume anyone is telling you the truth, and always *always* try the water before you buy (assuming you are buying a property with an existing well and plumbing). Your next step is to keep on talking to that potential neighbor. Get specific. What issues are they experiencing with water? Remember that your potential neighbor might be interested in your property too, and have an interest in talking you out of *your* interest. Follow up with a trip to the local county or borough seat and have a look at their records, or ask the recorder for their two cents. If water scarcity is a potential issue, find the APN (assessor's parcel number) for the property you are interested in and talk to the local water and electrical providers. What would it take to get water or power service on your property? Even if you know you want to live fully off-grid, these conversations might give you some useful insight into the long-term viability of your homestead, should you buy this property (and it's never a bad feeling to know you have a potential backup should you need it). Off the record, these utility folks may have useful information about the water supply in your area.

Did you make contact with that local well driller with the best reputation in town? You've got two questions for him: How hard is it going to be to get water, and how good will the water be once I get it? Finally, when you walk the property, take a few empty plastic bottles with you, fill them using any water source you find, and do some testing.

BACTERIA, AMOEBAS, AND ALGAE

Your number one test, before you take a sip of that sparkling stream, should be for total coliform (TC) in drinking water. Total coliform refers to a large group of coliform bacteria, both fecal (pathogen-causing) and nonfecal. E. coli is one of the most prevalent forms of fecal coliform. Nonfecal coliform may be found in soil, animals, plants, and so on. If coliform is present in the water, it may be an indicator that potentially harmful pathogens are present in your water. Measures must be taken to locate the source of contamination prior to drinking your well water.

Another contaminant that is present in most surface water is giardia, which is the most common intestinal infection in human beings, globally (two hundred million cases per year). Giardia is a cyst-shaped parasite that can be found in soil with deposits of human or animal waste. Giardia knows no limits: It may be found within the confines of the city in municipal wastewater, or in the backcountry in lakes, ponds, streams, and rivers. As beavers are heavily distributed throughout Alaska's lakes and ponds, giardia (commonly known as "Beaver Fever") is an ever-present concern for us. We've worked with homesteaders who had been drinking giardia-infested water for years, and dealing with the attending health issues for the same length of time.

Recently, toxic blue-green algae has been in the news. This algae is found in freshwater ponds, and in high concentrations can kill dogs and can cause serious illness in children.

The easiest way to avoid bacteria, algae, or amoebas is to avoid them altogether, bypassing streams and rivers and getting your water from a spring—ensuring it has no runoff and isn't being used as a water source by animals. Second to a spring is digging a well. Third is a solution we'll discuss in more depth in a few pages: UV light.

METALS

Most untreated drinking water has some natural metals in it. Not all are bad news: calcium (for instance) in reasonable quantities is good news for bones and teeth. However, *heavy metals* like cadmium, lead, mercury, and chromium (among others) are serious trouble. Drinking lead and mercury can lead to autoimmune diseases, in which your body begins to attack its own cells. Eventually this can lead to diseases like rheumatoid arthritis or problems with the kidneys, the circulatory system, or the nervous system. All heavy metals can lead to learning difficulties, aggressive behavior, hyperactivity, memory problems, stunted growth, or nerve damage.

One potential indicator of metals in the water is discoloration, either of the water itself or of the sinks, taps, and bathroom fixtures. (Note: There are plenty of benign reasons why this may happen, such as tannins that turn water brown.) If you suspect heavy metals in your water, take a sample and send it to the local toxicology lab. They'll be able to give you the information you need to decide if it's worth the risk or not. Remember: Even if you come up with another source of drinking water for yourself, it's a reasonable bet that anything you raise or grow on the land is going to be absorbing these metals as they graze or grow. If you eat these vegetables or meat products, you may be consuming potentially harmful metals. There are multiple ways to test your water. Most kits are priced under three hundred dollars, with a week or so turnaround. I get that most homesteaders are working on a budget, but if it saves you from buying land with dangerously contaminated water it will be the best three hundred you've ever spent.

UNPREDICTABLE WATER SUPPLY

Most of our water supply, at least in the western states, is underground, in huge reservoirs called aquifers. When rain falls, it percolates down into the soil and eventually is collected and stored in these underground sponges. Groundwater supplies 25 to 40 percent of global drinking water. Yet most of the water is used by agriculture (around 70 percent) or, increasingly, data storage centers: Each one of these concrete boxes sprouting up across the American Southwest uses between 360,000 and eight million gallons of groundwater *a day* for cooling.

All of this is to say that competition for water has never been more intense than it is now. So when water does come, in the form of monsoon rains, you need to hold on to every drop.

After all, the west is dry—until it isn't. We worked with an elderly couple in Arizona who endured drought-like conditions for ten months out of the year, and sporadic monsoon floods the other two months of the year. In the next chapter we'll talk about how we helped fortify their homestead against flash flooding. But for now, we had to help them to take advantage of these sudden downpours and collect as much of that water as possible.

In the long run, you want to create a homestead that soaks up sudden rainfalls and allows them to percolate into the ground, ideally replenishing the aquifers, or filtering through to emerge from springs or seeps. One of the best ways to do this is through regenerative agriculture—a long name for something most homesteaders are doing instinctively anyway. Commercially farmed soil is stripped bare of earthworms and microbial and insect life. This soil becomes loose and powdery, incapable of holding moisture and blowing away in storms or bad weather (think of the Dust Bowl and how it stripped topsoil from the Central Great Plains). We'll talk more about this in the gardening chapter, but for now understand that one big part of this approach is to improve the soil so that it is capable of storing water, and allowing it to slowly seep into the ground rather than racing away in a flash flood.

WATER RIGHTS

Finally, you need to understand just who owns the water in the area you are interested in. If you're looking to settle east of the 100th Meridian (the north-south axis that cuts down through the Dakotas, Nebraska, Kansas, and Oklahoma, and through Dallas and Austin), water rights are not a hugely difficult issue to solve—for the simple reason that in most cases there's enough water for everyone. Water rights are managed through a system based on property rights (after the old English idea of riparian rights), which assumes that there is a reasonable amount of water flowing naturally and that a drought is unlikely.

West of the meridian? Well, that's drier . . . and more complicated. Early western settlers saw water as a communal resource that wasn't permanently allocated to any particular group or individual but was shared based on the needs of the moment. This changed in the late 1800s, with the Gold Rush Mining Act of 1866, when a set of mining laws specifying lode (veins of mineral deposits in rock), ditch, and canal rights (1866) later combined with the Placer Law of 1871 (mineral deposits in water) to form the General Mining Act of 1872, granting miners the rights to survey and stake claims on public lands without prior ownership of the property. (Public lands refers to both land and waterways.)

This idea is called prior appropriation, and it's shaped the US west ever since because "while no one may own the water in a stream, all persons, corporations, and municipalities have the right to use the water for beneficial purposes." The most important thing you need to understand is that just because you have flowing water on your property, it doesn't mean you have the right to use it.

WESTERN WATER

Here's a tale of two Montana neighbors . . . and three property lines. Think of the capital letter *T* and picture our homesteader's property on the left of the vertical line. The neighbors above him (sitting on the horizontal line) had given him permission to tap into their spring, allowing him to gravity feed the five-hundred-gallon water tank inside his cabin. However, relationships between neighbors can go south, and in that one year they had cut his water supply off . . . twice. Ever hear of the Hatfields and McCoys? Exactly. Neighbors happen, and you have to work with the neighbors you have.

Our homesteader could see a spring, twenty feet from the property line *on his other neighbor's side* (think of the horizontal line of the T). With water that close, he was convinced there was water somewhere on his ten acres. I wasn't. But I was willing to get an excavator delivered, and I asked him where he wanted me to dig for any signs of water. Two days and four dry holes later, stark desperation descended over the ten dry acres. Facing the geological facts logically, I began looking for a large water tank to put on his larger flatbed truck, as hauling water from town was the only guarantee I could give him in his quest to be self-reliant, should the neighbors cut his water off for the third time, or worse, permanently.

But while setting this plan in motion I could see a year-round spring trickling into a six-foot-diameter pool of water, two feet deep, just twenty feet away. So close, but legally, so far. It was on the neighbor's land. I decided to dig a deep hole on the edge of his property line, as deep as the excavator arm would reach. In less than an hour I was eighteen feet deep, but no water. Believe me, I've been here before, many times. Digging through gravel in Colorado, tundra in Alaska, shale in Idaho, clay in Missouri, sand in Georgia, and so on. And all while anxious (and thirsty) homesteaders strain their eyes seeking signs of water in every excavated scoop of dirt. I truly empathize with and want to help people in their respective dreams of living self-sufficiently. But I'm also fully aware that the search for water (especially in desert regions) is always a gamble, and although this homesteader lived in Horseshoe Valley, the folklorish good luck symbol wasn't living up to its legend.

As luck wouldn't have it, our eighteen-foot-deep hole in the ground was bone-dry. I had intentionally dug deeper in elevation than the pool of water twenty feet away, hoping there was a chance that our deeper hole would allow water to gravitate downward and seep over to our side of the property line. One can hope.

Early the next morning I returned to the dig site to see if the Hail Mary effort had produced water. Nothing. And then, as we were both standing there awkwardly accepting our losses, the homesteader tells me that the pool of water is in his actual, legal driveway easement (from the top of his property going "right" down the horizontal line of the T that is shared with his neighbor above him). Wait . . . what the . . . ? This breaking-news flash would allow me to put in a new, deeded, legal driveway, and more importantly, most likely access some water on the way. Immediately I see in my head how I'll execute a plan that would give this guy water before the sun sets. Or not . . .

As I share the idea with the homesteader, he tells me the neighbors don't want him to put in this legal driveway, partly because they like the trees that would have to be cut, and second, they actually use *his* existing driveway to bring in large trucks or trailers, as their driveway entrance has a tight turn making it difficult for large vehicles to navigate. What? I sit the homesteader down and explain to him (things I'm sure he already knows) that he has the legal right to put in this new driveway, and most likely get water out of the deal. In this conversation I find out that there's yet another neighbor (whose property line is to the right of the vertical line of the T) who owns the actual property that this possible new driveway would run through. (Hatfield . . . or McCoy?)

Please note that my homesteader guy (single father of two kids, six and ten) just might be the nicest guy on earth. Impressively nice. So nice that I could see it would be difficult for him to approach the neighbor with my invasive "build a legal driveway and get some water" plan.

What would you do if you had springs on your property and your neighbor, who had none, asked you for permission to use those springs? I was playing this out in my head in both scenarios. Much like the homesteader, it would be real hard for me to ask my neighbor (or anyone) for help, and I'd be thinking the whole time that the answer would be no anyway, so why ask?

And then, as the owner of those life-giving springs, would I be generous and neighborly enough to give permission to someone in need (in this case, a single dad with two very young daughters)? I tell you now, if I had a neighbor like this guy I would have already approached him with an offer to help. And as life would have it, I'm not the only one.

When the homesteader stepped over his property line (and beyond his comfort zone), reluctantly informing those neighbors what we were up to, they came over to weigh in. They were younger and had been in the valley longer. They expressed to me how much they liked my homesteader, and had watched him from day one determinedly scratch out his homesteading dream. In just a few minutes' time, this young couple devised a plan far better than mine. They asked me if it was possible to dig a pond big enough to benefit both properties, essentially erasing the property line, where both landowners could enjoy water and recreation, and end up with a reservoir for the forestry department to use in case of forest fires (this is country that's at extremely high risk). I was leaving in forty-eight hours, so I immediately began digging on the young couple's property. The ground was crushed rock, rather than clay. Not good, since it would allow the water to seep out of the pond. So we contacted the owner of a pond liner company in Oregon, and after a producer explained my plight, he offered to donate us a 70' by 60' commercial liner and personally deliver it to Horseshoe Valley, Montana. Not only was this a seven-thousand-dollar gift, it was a 1,600-mile round-trip free delivery!

Meanwhile I roughed out the oval pond's footprint, constantly consulting the young couple, making sure we were all on the same page. The next morning the pond liner arrived, and I was informed it would take seven people to unravel, stretch, and place it into the pond's cavity. Not to worry. The local neighbors came out of the woodwork to help out this humble, quiet, nice homesteader. In less than an hour, the liner was in place, and two hours later the perimeter was secured with gravel.

As we sat back and watched, two 4" pipes from the spring trickled in clear mountain spring water. Some quick math deduced that once full, we all would be looking at 150,000 gallons of water. We did finish some metal roofing on the cabin in preparation for future rain catchment, but honestly that pales to insignificance when considering the spring's annual potential of three hundred thousand gallons, conservatively. The spring will produce twice as much water annually than the pond can hold at full capacity. Unbelievable. (A spillway was created to disperse overflow.)

During our nine-day stay, Misty, Matt, and the extended crew built a greenhouse. Now those plants and animals have an abundant water supply, allowing this homesteader to survive and thrive successfully. To date, he is still getting water from the good neighbor above him, and thanks to the good neighbors beside him (the young couple), his once-dry ten acres now has its own water source for eternity.

One fourth of this 70' by 60' pond extends onto the homesteader's land, but should the neighbors above him shut off the water, or someday sell to someone named Hatfield, or if the young couple sell their property to a McCoy, it's not going to matter. Why? This pond will forever be a testament to something stronger and longer-lasting than any feud. It underscores the benefits of neighbor helping neighbor.

It's easy to become jaded in these ever-changing times, but what I witnessed firsthand in Montana moved me. I was reminded that in this homesteading community, good still exists. Just before I jumped in the truck to leave, I asked the homesteader's ten-year-old daughter, Blaze, "Hey, I'm leaving in one minute, is there anything else I can do for you guys before I leave?" Catching her off guard, I could see her actually thinking if there was really anything else we could do to help them more. Then she said, "No, I think we're . . . good."

And Miss Blaze, if you ever read this, I couldn't agree more with you, little darlin'.

BACK IN ALASKA

If you want good, safe water, you may need to get creative. And, just when you think everything is settled, and your water supply is in good shape, you may need to get creative *again*. This is the heart of homesteading, and I've learned it over and over again on my own properties.

My own property is covered in four feet of snow every winter. So water should be no problem, right? Wrong! It's taken a few different approaches to find a clean, potable, safe, and reliable water source. Both the stream and the river were out of the question due to our local "neighbors" (i.e., their droppings). Instead of investing in expensive filtration equipment, I looked for a spring that was guaranteed to be contaminant-free. Early on we found a year-round spring seeping out of a bank near the edge of the river. I watched it closely and was pleasantly surprised to see it running at 35 degrees below zero. Amazing. We dug it out just enough to drop in a forty-five-gallon barrel. Inside the immersed barrel, I set a 110-volt submersible well pump. I then ran a seven-hundred-foot, one-inch water line uphill to the cabin. Inside the cabin was a three-hundred-gallon storage tank, which we filled once a week. This was a simple, straightforward year-round water source, but not without its issues. The line was above ground, and we had to make sure it was completely empty of water between fillings. The line had a fifty-foot rise from the spring to the cabin, which allowed gravity to drain it. I fought it for two winters, then our cabin burned down on winter number three.

My plan for the fourth winter was to dig for water next to the cabin (abandoning the spring) with the excavator, hoping to hit water twenty feet down and have a buried, insulated water line pumping water straight into the cabin's pressure tank. Two inches of rigid blue board buys you the same insulation as two feet of dirt. Plastic on top of the blue board assists in protecting the water line from freezing. It captures the geothermal ground temperature of around 55 degrees, and serves as a barrier should frost reach the plastic.

But when the fire burned all that we owned to the ground, we relocated 250 feet above our original homestead cabin site.

Our forty-acre homestead is split right down the middle with a two-hundred-foot-tall, near-vertical granite cliff. The upper twenty is high and dry, and most important, it receives every critical ray of valuable winter sun. For twenty-five years, since the purchase of the forty, everyone said accessing those twenty clifftop acres was impossible. I believed them. I had talked with some dynamite guys (powder monkeys) about blasting out our road on top, but it was cost-prohibitive for me to pursue.

A firm believer in "Don't quit before you start," I bought an older 200 Hitachi excavator, walked it across the sketchy Little Susitna River (the track came off in the river, a two-hour fix), and headed for the base of the cliffs. Three extremely dangerous days later, the excavator broke out on top, breaching the impossible cliffs, opening up the future of this homestead. However, while clawing, scratching, and inching my way to the top, I hit three seeps of water. I definitely footnoted that for future intel. Was there actually a reservoir of water trapped in the bedrock on top of a 250-foot cliff? Again, I could stand there dormant in disbelief, or fire up the excavator and start prospecting. Not good. The first two holes I dug were bone-dry and only ten feet deep, as I had struck impenetrable bedrock. But on the third try, there it was. The game changer. The life changer. Water. I dug a twenty-foot-deep hole, dropped in a 48"-diameter culvert twenty feet long vertical, and waited for water to seek its natural level. Two days later, around 1,200 gallons of pure, unadulterated mountain spring water became our new life-sustaining water source. I installed a 220-volt submersible pump and dug an eight-foot-deep water line five hundred feet to the cabin. I covered the water line with blue board insulation and placed a layer of 6 mil plastic over it. All the while, still in disbelief that water would ever be found up there. Miracle.

But had I not gone against the conventional wisdom of armchair quarterbacks and thrown the Hail Mary pass, I would not have gotten to this amazing new log cabin location, nor would I have found this priceless water. Look before you leap, but definitely still leap.

> Look before you leap, but definitely still leap.

Many homesteaders are faced with water challenges and fall back on hauling it in from town. But believe it or not, on at least five homesteads (including ours), I found water that they had no idea was there. Don't give up. Ever.

CHOOSING YOUR WATER SYSTEM

As you build your water system, bear in mind you may have to combine one or more of these ideas to create a reliable water source. For instance, you may end up using a vacuum pump, spring box, and UV filter within one water system. Look out for ways nature can help you. Hills are your friend, so scout for a spring or seep on a hill above your property. Remember that in an ideal scenario you want to keep your water moving, not stagnant, with enough flow that an overflow pipe can carry water away from a tank or spring box rather than letting it stand. A constant supply of fresh water will prevent the build-up of sediments or bacteria, as well as simply taste better too.

If city water is an option, you may be tempted to tap into that simple resource. Not necessarily a bad idea, but one that leaves you vulnerable to catastrophic or unexpected events like a big earthquake or even a cyberattack. If you do go the city water route, consider having a backup plan on your property. At the very least make sure you have rain barrels filled and ready to use at all times.

You will most likely be modifying, improving, and refining your water system for as long as you are living on the homestead. Do what you can with the budget you have, and improve it as you are able to.

DIG YOUR WELL

We've mentioned "your local well digger" a few times so far. *Well*, now's the time to make that call. As I've said, a good well digger is worth his weight in gold, a.k.a. water. He or she will know your area well and be able to give you a reasonable assessment, both of the cost of digging and the probability of hitting the wet stuff. Your well will be one of the most expensive investments you make, so take time to find the right person. One homesteader that you've seen on your TV screen spent more than forty thousand dollars total to get water to their cabin. The well, the pump, and the trench . . . Again, do your homework. Worse: Shallow water is more likely to be contaminated by runoff or other commercial contaminants (something you need to consider if you are drilling a well in areas with fracking, mining, or industrial farming). A deeper well offers better filtration, since the water has had to seep down through more layers of sediment, earth, and sand.

Once you've dug your well, you'll need to get the water out of it. Plenty of homesteaders rely on the hand pump system, and, frankly, generations of homesteaders did just fine using one. But this kind of strenuous activity can be dangerous for older or medically frail homesteaders (we met one family whose patriarch had died while hand pumping water). An electric pump will make your life simple and easy—so long as the power stays on.

HYDRAULIC, VACUUM, OR RAM PUMPS

Let's say your water source for your property is a stream located downhill from your home. Not ideal, but sometimes that's just the way it is. How are you going to get your water up that hill, into your house, and out of your taps? A motorized pump is best, but there is also an older, nonmotorized system that will use the water's own power to propel it uphill. These hydraulic pumps have been around for hundreds of years, and use the power of inertia to pump water out of a stream. Even better, it is possible to build one

Ram pump: Rest assured, ram pumps have been working since . . . 1796.

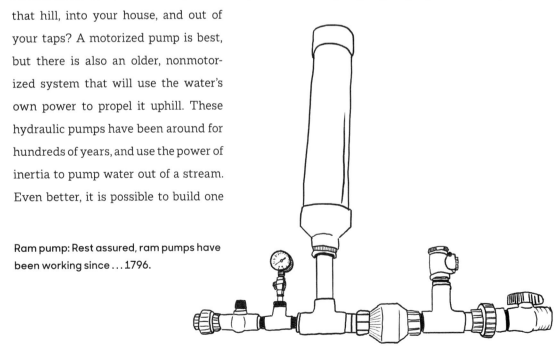

yourself, out of parts accessible from any hardware store that sells plumbing/pipe fittings. So long as your stream—and the hill—meet a few parameters (the stream has to have sufficient flow, the ram pump can't be more than one hundred feet from the stream, and the uphill leg of the pump can't be too far from the pump), the hydraulic or vacuum pump can deliver a thin but steady trickle of water. Assuming you are collecting it in a rain barrel, you will have enough water for the domestic needs of your household. There are extensive plans for a DIY ram pump online, as well as the mathematical formulas necessary to ensure you have correctly calibrated it.

RAIN CATCHMENT

Imagine living on a property where you have all the water you need, and every drop falls from the sky. This system is referred to as rain catchment, and it does just that. After the rain falls on your roof, it runs down past the roof's edge into gutters, where continuous enclosed downspouts or plastic pipes transfer the captured water into some form of water storage.

Water catchment is a legitimate, proven way to live fully in a region lacking water. Why? Because in states such as Arizona and New Mexico, rain comes in monsoons—intense summer storms that dump significant amounts of water in short bursts. That elderly couple in rural Arizona could provide for all their water needs with effective catchment. And here's another thought: Water catchment isn't limited solely to tanks, cisterns, and gutters. Part of effective water catchment is fortifying the soil with deep-rooted trees that cool the air and ground, lessen evaporation, and improve soil drainage and percolation (the last thing you want to see is that precious water, unabsorbed by hard, compacted soil, racing off your property—most likely taking your equally precious topsoil with it).

We live in an information overload world, and in less than one minute, you could type in your property and ask the annual rainfall, even down to its respective months. As you consider your new property investment, do the math on how much rainfall you can expect, and how you can collect it.

It's not uncommon to see million-dollar homes in Hawaii using this system. Why? Because each of the eight Hawaiian Islands has a "wet" side, which translates to rain forest. Arid areas need all the rain catchment they can get, using the same exact system. Slanted roofs. Gutters. Storage.

In Ohio, the Broadheads built a spacious home out of thirty thousand used tires, ending up with a three-thousand-square-foot slanted metal roof. (For catchment, I recommend a metal roof, even though any type of roofing material will still be susceptible to contamination from trees, birds, squirrels, and more.)

How much rainwater can that roof capture for them? Here's a simple formula. One inch of rain falling on a one-thousand-square-foot roof can produce approximately six hundred gallons of water. So for every one inch of rain falling on the Broadheads' significant three-thousand-square-foot roof area, it would equate to 1,800 gallons per inch.

Once again, "dew" diligence comes into play. Nevada law recently changed: After years of not allowing rain catchment, households are now allowed "de minimis collection." This means the rainfall from one single-family dwelling may be collected, but not used for domestic consumption. Great for your garden, not so great to supplement your drinking water supply. In Colorado, you are allowed two barrels, totaling 110 gallons per house. In Utah you need a permit, and there's a 2,500-gallon maximum harvest. Ohio has some codes and restrictions on rain catchment. Do your research to find the dos and don'ts of water catchment for each of the fifty states. The "H_2Onus" is on you.

With twelve thousand rivers and three million lakes, water catchment in Alaska is a nonissue. But choosing to live in desert areas like (and certainly not limited to) Arizona, New Mexico, Texas, and Nevada, you'll definitely need to know your average rainfall, keeping in mind summers seem to be getting hotter and droughts more common.

Please note, even where water is plentiful, it's nice to have catchment on outbuildings, such as barns, pens, coops, etc., instead of running unsightly garden hoses "over hill and dale." It's convenient, at least during nonwinter months, to have fifty-five gallons of water available 24/7 at the edge of an outbuilding's roof (and if you ever have a small fire, you'll be glad you did this).

Anyone wanting to live in a yurt or geodesic dome in regions where off-gridders (and on-gridders) have long relied on rain catchment from traditional roof designs to survive and thrive may note it's difficult to install straight gutters on a round structure. (Why did the preacher build a round church? So the Devil couldn't corner him.) Round hole, square peg. Water is life; without it, it's strife.

Finally, remember what I said about the benefits of keeping water flowing? Rain catchment is more susceptible to contamination because it is stored in cisterns and doesn't circulate. Make sure your system is lidded to prevent mosquito infestation (if there's a half-inch hole in any size tank, any flying thing or crawling thing will find its way into your drinking water, guaranteed). Empty your tanks and clean them regularly. And don't drink the water without treating it first; rain is pure, but your roof is not. One young couple in Missouri found out the hard way that their tanks were contaminated with insects and essentially undrinkable. The Broadheads have full cisterns, but will need to treat any water used for drinking.

SPRING BOXES

Many a homesteader has thrived using a spring box as their water source. This is a concrete or wooden surround built to capture and hold ten or twenty gallons of water from a spring, generally positioned where the homesteaders have installed a water line to bring that water to the homestead. We showed up in Tennessee and found a couple struggling to get by in a camper perched on a steep driveway. They were hauling water, but their property had a stream running through the middle of it. We eventually built them a 16' by 16' cabin higher up the mountain on a flat-ish spot. While I was trying to figure out a way to install a UV

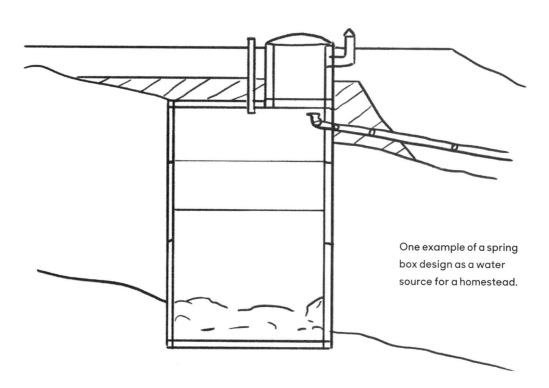

One example of a spring box design as a water source for a homestead.

system, which would make their stream safer to drink, Misty discovered a very small trickle seeping out of the ground one hundred feet above their new home site. She developed it by drilling rebar into the flow's bedrock and laying up a concrete block catchment. She put an aromatic cedar lid on it and piped that mountain water to the cabin. Since the spring box was much higher in elevation than their new home, they had a gravity-fed water supply, requiring zero pumps or electrical power.

CISTERNS

In Season One of *Homestead Rescue* we worked with a couple who had settled in a remote part of Montana who had everything except water (which means they had nothing . . .). There were no springs, no streams, and precious little rainfall. Digging a well wasn't an option due to the hard, rocky ground. The husband was driving hundreds of miles multiple times a week to fill up small tanks in the back of his pickup. Not only was lack of water a problem, so was lack of husband, as the wife tried to do the daily chores and add new projects on the homestead solo. We couldn't make a natural source of water appear, but we could help the couple by creating a man-made source of water on the property. On the second to last day of the shoot, we dug a large hole and put a five-thousand-gallon cistern in it. We filled in the rest of the hole with dirt, making sure the water would not be exposed to sunlight, and had a tanker come and fill it with H_2O. Personally, I wouldn't want to set up a homestead on a property without a natural water supply. However, a cistern will take that kind of property from unlivable to functional. The homesteaders still need to purchase water—and pay a tanker to deliver it—on a monthly basis, but having the husband at home with his wife, working the land, is priceless.

GRAVITY-FED WATER SYSTEM

In Vermont we found a nice, well-educated couple who had been living in a uniquely built straw-bale house since 2016 who were also packing water from a stream on their property. I tested their water, and I didn't like the results. They also had no vehicle access to their home (no bridge), and that same significant stream was the reason. Preoccupied with a bridge build, I was also determined to find them safer water before we left. They had a very sketchy, weak solar-power system and I didn't want to add more stress to it (or them) by adding an electric pump should I find water. I had a large excavator on site and on the second-to-last day (bridge/driveway to front door completed . . . whew), I pointed the excavator up the mountain, following steep, thirty-year-old "log skidder" roads. The goal was to find a spring above their cabin, providing a free (of electricity) gravity-fed water source with a bonus of water pressure. (Water running downhill can build pressure. The higher the fall, the more the pressure. Most likely the electricity in your home is powered by this same principle. Water is captured behind a dam. Then that water falls downhill, inside the dam, propelling turbines that generate electricity.)

I dug six holes and all were bone-dry. I came down from the high ground, and on the seventh hole I hit a significant spring. I immediately dug a four-hundred-foot long, five-foot-deep water line to the cabin. We were due to leave the homestead at four p.m. to catch our next flight, but I got the excavator stuck and had a few other things go wrong in my haste. At dark, we left them with fifty gallons of water in a crude but effective plastic potable water catchment that was about seven feet higher than their kitchen sink. Boom! Gravity-fed water. We plumbed the house for hot and cold water, introducing an on-demand propane-fired hot water unit scavenged from a motorhome. I'm hoping right now they are drinking from that spring box, and perhaps enjoying a hot bath for the first time since . . . 2016.

BEHIND THE SCENES

We successfully built them a bridge that safely supported a thirty-thousand-pound excavator, a driveway from the bridge to the house, a geothermal greenhouse, a new metal roof on their cabin, three separate partitioned, private bedrooms in their cabin loft, a stone bear-proof compost container, a gravity-fed water system, and a few other things.

This wrapped two episodes in a row, and everyone in production was spent. The next morning I got up at six and headed to the homestead. No cameras. No crew. No one. I jumped on the excavator and spent four hours on the road system side of their new bridge/access driveway. They needed a new approach to drive straight onto the bridge. This required a new driveway entry. I'd say it was fifty yards and miraculously I found gravel on site. I dug a huge hole, spread out the gravel, and put the tree stumps, limbs, and debris back into the hole. I had to drive to Albany, New York, from Killington, Vermont, and catch a plane home to Alaska. I worked right up to the very last minute and the second I got done, here came the homesteaders back from town. I broke out my phone and captured them pulling into their brand-new driveway, crossing their very own bridge, and parking at their front door for the very first time. They walked back down to the bridge. She gave me a heartfelt hug, and he shook my hand. Clint and I dang near missed the plane back to Alaska. Close one.

BEFORE YOU DRINK THAT WATER

Finally, just because you have water doesn't necessarily mean you want to drink it. Remember those bacteria we talked about at the beginning of the chapter? Even well water can be contaminated by them, so before you turn on the tap, install a purification system that will guarantee a safe glass to drink. There are two main systems, described here.

CHLORINE VS. ULTRAVIOLET

Here's how it usually plays out: A new property owner, at some point, will have their water tested. And far too often, those results will find coliform and E. coli bacteria in their drinking water. Especially any surface water, such as that from springs, lakes, and rivers. That leads the homeowner down the "How do I make my drinking water safer?" path. Just a few steps into that journey you find a fork in the trail: One way says chlorine, the other says ultraviolet (UV).

Spoiler alert: I'll tell you now, UV is the better path. Why?

In the 1800s, cholera was a deadly, terrifying, highly transmissible, and much feared disease. Most people believed that "miasma" coming from decomposing matter was the cause of the infection. In 1854, a British physician realized that all his cholera patients had used the same pump in a poor part of London and he put two and two—or billions and billions of microbes—together. He then discovered chlorine was an effective way to disinfect water. And today, more than 70 percent of all Americans are drinking tap water, most likely treated with chlorine. But studies since then have found out that long-term consumption of water treated with chlorine is indeed harmful to humans. Let me count the ways: asthma, food allergies, congenital abnormalities, various types of cancer, and an unpleasant taste and smell.

Chlorine works quickly and thoroughly as it attacks the tissue of microorganisms and bacteria, but it actually goes one step too far as it also affects the good things in your water. In that overkill process, chlorine affects the naturally occurring chemicals in your water, and that end result can introduce harmful disinfection by-products into your glass of water.

UV, on the other hand, kills 99.99 percent of all microbes present in your water system. But to operate efficiently, your water coming into the UV component must be clean. If it isn't, you will need to put a filter in front of it, meaning on the intake side of the unit. UV light works by breaking apart oxygen molecules; these molecules reform into O_3, or ozone. Ozone is a powerful disinfectant, killing most bacteria and viruses. UV introduces nothing harmful to your water, and doesn't affect its taste.

So I recommend you take the path saying "UV": You may have to pick up a filter along the way, but hey, a nice, clean, cold, safe glass of water awaits you at the end of the trail. Keep in mind, most people on this planet have no say in how their water is treated for safety; you do.

WATER IS LIFE

Every indicator is that water, at least in the western states, is going to get harder to find and more competitive to claim. A lot of people got very wealthy rerouting water away from smaller, older communities into big profitable towns and industries. Water has transformed inhospitable deserts into megacities like Phoenix, Los Angeles, and Las Vegas. The water may be disappearing, but these huge population centers aren't going anywhere. This doesn't have to derail your homestead dreams. Throughout the last nine seasons of *Homestead Rescue* we've met people using their wits, ingenuity, and energy to bring the stuff of life to their property. Frankly, no one impressed me more with their grit and determination than the Kondor family of Nevada.

Twenty-nine-year-old Kaleb Kondor paid six thousand dollars for a forty-acre tract of Nevada desert. His parents had fallen on hard times in Reno and ultimately lost the family home to the bank. They were now homeless. Kaleb purchased two circa-1970s camp trailers, one for his parents and one for his sixteen-year-old brother. Kaleb's finances limited his noble pursuit. It was the best he could do for his family. Every attempt to progress their new off-grid homestead was thwarted by severe heat, incessant wind, and a property without . . . water.

Water was hauled in forty-five-gallon barrels from Lovelock, Nevada, a town in the midst of an eight-year drought. Determined to succeed, they planted three hundred fruit trees, as well as a garden. Within months, the fruit trees had all died. The garden, ravaged by wind, failed.

A desert is a desert. Hot. Dry. Harsh. Uninhabitable . . . for most.

Kaleb reached out to me for help. I accepted, and found myself on the homestead a few days later. The homestead had an aura of desperation. It hung in the air. It swirled in the dust devils and stared back at me as the family recapped their last two years of struggle.

The cost is fifty dollars per foot to drill a water well in this area. Expensive. I found the most experienced (second-generation) driller in the valley and drove him out to the homestead. It took him less than one minute to give me his opinion: "The best thing this family can do for themselves is to pack up and move back to Reno. There's no water in these mountains." Bad news, and I believed him . . .

The next day I located a heavy-duty military trailer that would haul a thousand gallons of water, as the Kondors had a brand-new thousand-gallon water tank on the property. Empty. This would make for fewer trips to town and, as the tank was brand-new, it was far more sanitary than the barrels I saw in the back of the family truck, all of which required cleaning. It was the best I could do for this family. Or was it?

On day one of my visit, Kaleb showed me a murky, muddy, pungent puddle of water two feet in diameter and a few hundred yards from his western property line. Coyote and deer tracks peppered the edge of this barely visible watering hole. I've dealt with this same scenario in Alaska: someone building on a mountainside, gambling on finding water. Five-hundred-foot dry wells are not uncommon. I've been fortunate; I own two wells each around 120 feet in depth, each producing pristine Alaskan water. But here on the Kondor homestead, the desperation was as high as the human spirit was low.

In the middle of this homestead was a huge, hand-dug hole, ten feet deep by six feet wide. I climbed down in it and scratched at the walls. Hardpan: tough digging. I could feel the hope in every shovelful of dirt taken out and the crushing despair of failure. *One* pick. *One* shovel. *One* homesteader: desperate, determined, unwavering. This hand-dug attempt to find water summed up the Kondor homestead in two words: rock bottom.

I was asked to help them, but was unsure if the water wagon fix was enough in the big picture. This is a good family. They deserved more from me, and quite frankly, I sensed they *expected* more from me. Against my better judgment and contrary to a certain seasoned well driller's advice, I committed to drill a fifty-dollar-per-foot, five-hundred-foot-deep well. Price tag? Twenty-five grand. I called the driller. He said, "Marty, I'll drill your five-hundred-foot well but I'm telling you in advance, we're not going to hit water. And one more thing: I'm keeping the twenty-five thousand." The Kondors were unaware of this last-ditch effort. As the massive drill rig rolled up to the homestead and the dust settled, the four Kondors stood there somewhere between disbelief and hope. I'm not a geologist, nor am I a hydrologist, but my thought process was this: drill at the exact elevation of the small watering hole across the valley. Was there an aquifer somewhere beneath this barren desert surface, running at this specific elevation? There was only one way to find out: I scratched an X in the middle of the Nevada desert with my cowboy boot and said, "Drill here." From that second on, I felt the weight of that family's future there bearing down on me.

DAY 1 of drilling: dry hole, no water. The driller didn't say a word as he jumped in his pickup and headed back to town. Solemn.

DAY 2 of drilling: dry hole, no water. At the end of the day, I called my longtime well-drilling friend in Alaska, Bob Friesen, apprising him of my plight. I only remembered one sentence from that half-hour phone call: "Marty, always listen to your well driller." Too late, Bob.

DAY 3 of drilling: I checked at noon. Dry hole, no water. So I went back to work. I was converting a steel shipping container (a Conex) into a tiny home for Kaleb's parents when I heard shouting. I stepped outside and saw Kaleb running across the desert toward the drill rig. He was followed by his parents and his younger brother. Was there an accident? Or . . . The desert wind, the drill rig noise, and the distance made it hard to hear what was happening, but something *was* happening. I recalled the driller telling me we wouldn't hit water in a million years. I responded, "So you're saying there's a chance?" He didn't laugh. As I closed the gap from the Conex to the drill rig, I heard shouting and laughing. And then I saw it: a crystal-clear flowing stream of . . . water *and* a shocked well driller looking at me, speechless. The Kondors were jumping up and down and tears flowed like . . . water, including my own. I witnessed a miracle on that mountain. He hit water at 160 feet, gushing at twenty gallons per minute. Clear. Drinkable. Enough water for ten homesteads. In one final spin of a drill bit, hope was restored to this deserving family. The unrealized dreams of the Kondor homestead became unfettered. An unlimited future lay wide open.

I thought of the Kondors as I struggled with finding drinkable water on our *own* homestead. A raging river prevented road access, so a well-drilling rig was not an option. The rivers and streams weren't necessarily safe to drink due to nearby beaver dams, salmon spawning grounds, bear scat, moose excrement, etc. Giardia is ubiquitous. Option? *One* pick. *One* shovel. *One* desperate, determined, unwavering homesteader.

The Kondors may see our friendship as one-sided, i.e., me saving them. But as I worked, shovelful after shovelful, I was inspired by Kaleb Kondor's will, grit, and backbone. A homesteader is only as good as his water supply, and the Kondors are a success story. Water is life.

FIVE

FLASH
FLOODS

Nearly every homesteader I've met has faced some form of flooding, but none more so than the residents of a small homestead in the Southwest. Ironically, the only lonely ol' dusty road to a dry, water-starved homestead in Saint John, Arizona,

Never underestimate the power of water.

would actually flash flood and trap them on the homestead side until the floodwaters subsided. Yep, deserts flood. And get anywhere near a stream, river, or lake during a torrential downpour and you'll be singin' "How high's the water, Mama?" In fact, in the five-year history of *Homestead Rescue*, the only time we didn't complete our homestead promises was in Missouri. Why? That hundred-year flood had taken out the main highways and even bridges, making it impossible to return to the homestead. The state of Missouri declared the affected area a national disaster. Seeing that unstoppable flooding up close and personal was impactful. Never underestimate the power of water, or hang ten on the edge of the Grand Canyon, which was shaped by the power of water over the millennia. The kicker is, buying in a floodplain zone is cheaper, and many a buyer has signed on the dotted line not knowing that their prospective home and property (and ultimately their dream) is uninsurable.

Flash floods are, according to the National Weather Service, the number one weather-related killer in the United States. And signs point to the rains getting more intense, and the flooding more severe, in the future. Here's an interesting relationship to wrap your head around: Even as the western US is getting drier and hotter, rains are likely to get more intense. Why? Because more heat in the environment = more energy. A hotter atmosphere means clouds hold more moisture. Hotter oceans and air lead to more evaporation, more cloud formation, and . . . eventually, more intense, long-lasting, and frequent storms as those cloud systems move east. California, Oregon, and Washington are also under increased threat from atmospheric rivers—plumes of intense moisture that function as rivers in the sky, dumping huge amounts of rain in short, very concentrated periods. Add this to severe drought conditions—and the dry, compacted, nonporous soils that come with them—and you have trouble.

Meanwhile, back on dry land, we've done our own part to increase flooding by building cities on floodplains (such as Houston) or other low-lying coastal areas. Compacted soils and paved-over roads, parking lots, and housing developments mean that when it does rain, the water has very few channels to escape, and becomes deeper, faster, and more volatile as it moves toward the coast. Some cities such as Miami are now experimenting with things like gravel parking lots to encourage percolation, but they are few and far between. In 2021, an area of rural Tennessee was left reeling from a "wall of water" that killed dozens. Germany was shocked over a flash flood that swept almost two hundred people to their deaths.

The reality is that five-hundred-year storms are likely to become regular events. So as you look for your property and begin to develop it, you need to have floods at the front of your mind.

WATER WEIGHT

In the last chapter we talked about how a gallon of water weighs 8.34 pounds. That adds up quickly when you're filling up tanks on the back of your pickup. It *really* adds up when you are talking about the energy fast moving water generates. A cubic foot of water weighs 62.4 pounds, and it moves downstream with great speed. Now, imagine you are driving down a rutted road, and you see a foot-high wave of muddy water moving toward you. It's tempting to believe you can outrun—maybe even drive straight through—the seemingly modest flood. It might only come to your shins, so what's the problem? Here's why that is such a terrible idea. Each foot of water will hit your car with five hundred pounds of force. Worse, for every foot that water rises, your car will become more buoyant and essentially "lose" 1,500 pounds of weight. Flash floods are deadly because they don't look as dangerous as they are. That water may only come up to your midshin, but it is more than enough to sweep away you, your car, and anyone else unfortunate enough to be in it.

Equally problematic: all the stuff that's *in* the water. Flash floods can cause two additional problems for the homesteader, washing away precious topsoil (the reason why the water is brown) and—even worse—spreading contaminants, such as farm runoff (gray or black water).

The easiest way to avoid being swept away in a flash flood is to understand the power of the flood itself. The second easiest way is to avoid areas prone to flash floods altogether. Not so simple these days: As I write this the city of Detroit is flooded. So are the subways of New York. South Texas has had twelve inches of rain in two days. And our friends in Arizona are hopefully enjoying the monsoons—now that their property is protected from the floods by the rock-filled culverts we installed for them.

There is a way to live safely in flood-prone areas, but it requires planning, knowledge, and a lot of hard work.

WILL THIS LAND FLOOD?

The easiest way to find out about your land's history of flooding—or otherwise—is to go to floodsmart.gov and enter the address or coordinates of the land you are looking at. Most insurance companies and real estate agents likewise have flood layers on their websites. And, of course, our standby—local knowledge. Yes, that potential neighbor may be getting tired of answering all of your questions, but "Does this land experience flash floods?" is an important one to ask. If your property is in what's called a hundred-year flood zone this is a red flag, both for the reasons outlined above and for the simple fact that damp land makes raising healthy animals and growing successful crops harder. Most homestead animals need dry land, simply to keep their feet healthy.

The past doesn't predict the future, however, so you need to look at the land with your own eyes as well. As you walk your potential property, look at any streams or rivers that run through it. You are looking at the topography: the way the water has cut through the land. Are there deep, ragged cuts along the riverbank? Are the riverbanks exposed, or covered in vegetation? Look at the soil along the river edge: fine silt, sand, or loose cobbles are indicative of prior floods. A debris line, either on the ground or in tree branches, is also an important indicator of recent flood activity. And finally, look at the structures on the property. Are there any indications of high-water marks on the walls, either exterior or interior? Has the soil been washed away around the foundations? Is there visible mold or a smell of mildew in the air? (I wrote a song titled "Do You Smell What We're Stepping In?"—a late-night honky-tonk metaphor, but it may literally apply in this paragraph.) Remember to look at usgs.gov for a wide variety of data and information about past floods. The information is out there, and it is well worth taking the time to assess flood risk on a property before you buy.

WHEN YOU ARE DETERMINED TO STAY

A few years back, the *Homestead Rescue* team showed up in Missouri to help an extended multigenerational family battling recurring floods, among other problems. The young homesteading couple showed me videos of floodwaters running down the valley, under and around their house (which was on stacked concrete blocks), and it looked like it ran at least two feet deep down the driveway where we were all standing. But was this flash flooding enough to make them relocate/move their home onto safer, higher ground on their parents' thirty acres? Nope. And I'm not sure if it was stubbornness or fear of potential damage to their first (only) home should we move it, but I didn't push the issue and looked at other options.

This family had one thing in common with homesteaders all over the country. They'd fought to buy their land. Every cabin, chicken coop, or greenhouse was a hard-earned victory that had taken years of work, and a lot of people pooling their income, to make it happen. My idea of reorganizing the homestead wasn't a bad one, but it wasn't the *right* one for them. We needed to find a way for this family to live safely, while still living where and how they wanted to.

After walking the higher ground above their cabin, I wondered if I could create a pond to capture the floodwaters, and should that succeed, create swales to control any excess overflow and redirect all threatening waters away from life and property. Well aware that Missouri is the only state that has stopped us from fulfilling a completed *Homestead Rescue* assignment due to catastrophic flooding, I had to think this through. Should I "imagineer" a pond, it would also serve as a dam . . . above their home? Build it wrong, and the dam could break, washing their home and their homestead dream downstream.

The first order of business was to dig down and find clay, because a thick layer of clay serves as nature's pond liner. Much like a commercial rubber membrane, clay's composition can pack so tight that water can't seep through. Having worked extensively throughout the Midwest, I knew there was a good chance clay was beneath the heavily treed surface. Full disclosure: Driving to this homestead, I spotted half a dozen homemade ponds, pushed out by bulldozers. The ponds were all full to their grassy brim, lined with happy, healthy (quenched) Black Angus cattle. Not every property in Missouri has soils that will allow you to create a pond, but multiple ponds close to their property hedged my bet, and after clearing trees I began mining for clay. Lo and behold, there it was—clay mixed with dirt, but hopefully enough to line the surface of this cavernous hole above their cabin. A few days later when I finished, it rained enough to capture about two feet of water in the pond. Whew. It was holding water. The entire family came to inspect it, and all weighed in on how they would use this fairly large pond once full: e.g., picnics, swimming, planting fish, and as a source of water for animals and gardens. But its primary purpose was to capture and control flash floods.

I decided to take it one step further and build an alarm on the overflow swale. I took a few cedar boards eight feet long and created a flume. At the downhill side of the inclined flume, I mounted an old bicycle rim complete with small sheet metal paddles, resembling a paddle wheel on the back of an old sternwheeler. I attached a couple of old Missouri license plates to the sides of the bicycle wheel's spokes, which rubbed against a wire hooked to a 12-volt car battery. Two wires ran from the battery to the side of their home, where the wires attached to an old horn pulled off an old 1970s F250 Ford pickup. This dam-side menagerie was to act as an alarm should floodwaters breach the dam's wall and run down the flume placed in the low spot of a control swale. The speed of the overflow would spin the paddled bicycle tire, and that movement would touch two wires fixed in place on each side of the tire. The license plates would drag along the fixed wire, making a 12-volt connection, basically honking the horn in the spinning process. It worked. In the end, we actually moved a 12' by 24' home addition into the "once upon a time" flood zone and set it next to their home, as this young couple wanted to grow a family. Who knows, by now they may have a couple of small children playing in the front yard of a homesite (instead of doing the backstroke in the backyard) that was once prone to flash floods. Or they may be having a family picnic, or swimming, or even catching bass for dinner.

FLOOD PROTECTION

You can't outrun or outmuscle a flash flood. Your best choice is to spend some time preparing your property to survive one. Ideally, you've bought land where your house is on an elevation, with no sparsely planted hills above it (ideal for funneling large amounts of water onto your property) and a good distance away from streams or rivers. In Hawaii we worked with an amazing couple, both world champion kite surfers, hardworking and smart. They built their house on the banks of a tranquil stream. But they had no idea that the looming mountain behind their property *and* the gully channeled those mountain rainfalls straight down to their "tranquil" stream. Everyone loves the sound of a stream at night until you find yourself knee-deep at midnight scrambling to save life and property.

THE FLOOD-PROOF HOME

As our weather gets more unpredictable, more and more land will become prone to flash flooding. But if you are still determined to build, consider these ideas. Look at the topography of your land: You want to be elevated, and out of any potential floodplains. That means if your land is flat and level with a nearby stream or river, you need to consider elevating your house. This sounds expensive, and it certainly can be. But successful homesteading relies on being creative and using materials already on the property rather than yet another four-figure Lowe's run. Back in Missouri—on another homestead—we elevated a simple cabin by using six large boulders as foundation "stilts." We drilled into the boulders, set rebar in them, and used said rebar to anchor the house down. These boulders gave the homesteaders roughly four feet of clearance from the ground. Now when the semi-regular floods come by, the water flows under the house, rather than through it.

AFTER THE FLOOD: BLACK MOLD

The one thing that stops me cold: mold! Here's a final thought to consider about your housing or other buildings: Just because your house survived a flood does not mean it's safe to re-inhabit. Black mold (Stachybotrys) or other kinds of mildew can be dangerous, even deadly. As eager as you may be to reclaim your home after a flood: stop. It's truly better for you and your family to live in a tent than in a home infected with black mold. We had a homesteading wife in Louisiana who was hospitalized due to black mold in the family's trailer. The homesteading community is full of DIY treatment plans and strategies. But even if you wipe down all surfaces with bleach, and treat the fungus with the various topical sprays sold at a hardware store, it's not enough. Essential-oil treatments, though popular with homesteaders, are insufficient. Even if they kill the mold, they leave behind the spores (mycotoxins), which can still be breathed in or ingested. Finally, visible black mold is a sure sign of invisible black mold, hidden in the drywall of your home. Just because you can't see it doesn't mean it's not there.

All of this adds up to a big problem, and one that there's no easy answer for. In Louisiana, we ended up condemning the trailer that the family was living in. Luckily, a local company stepped up and supplied a prefabricated home for the family. (This time we elevated it on a cinder-block foundation, mainly for safety in a storm, but also to allow for air circulation and limit the odds of flood damage.)

Most homesteaders aren't this lucky. Your best remedy for black mold is to build a home that limits the odds of an infection to begin with. Make sure there are no organics touching your home's exterior, such as grass, brush, or trees, as they introduce bugs and bacteria and provide a constant source of moisture. And, of course, always make sure that the grade around your house is sloping away. Any ground sloping toward your house will create dampened soil against your home's foundation. Installing 6 mil plastic on the ground before you pour concrete helps to prevent your concrete slab from wicking moisture from the ground to the surface. Remember that black mold loves wood and cellulose of all kinds. Most homesteaders are using wood to build their homes (we have multiple log cabins and I will talk about them in the next chapters). This means you have to take care to make your home as mold-resilient as possible. During the build, try to keep your materials dry (difficult, I get it). Store them off the ground and beneath waterproof tarps. Do your best to protect the build itself from rain, covering the entire structure with tarps if possible.

BACK IN ALASKA

Our forty acres in Alaska includes several acres of a beautiful Class IV river cascading through our southwest corner. It's my best friend and my worst enemy every day. I fall asleep each and every night of my life to its perpetual calming symphony, and wake every morning to its wild and commanding torrent. I love this river. I respect this river, and feel compelled to retract the unfriendly and untruthful statement I just expressed above. It will never be my worst enemy. Apologies to you, Little Susitna River. I'm in constant, daily awe of your beauty and power. You challenge me. You scare me. You force me to think. You make me work. You separate me from the world. After fifty years in Alaska, moving from Ketchikan, to Prince of Wales, to Haines, to Sitka, to Chugiak, to Wasilla, to Palmer, you've allowed only me and my family to cross your banks, and fulfill a lifelong dream. You've allowed us to live like Alaskans should live. And if I may be so worthy, someday, please, may you carry my ashes to the sea.

The Little Susitna is a scenic attraction complete with pullouts, viewing platforms, and a two-lane public road that mirrors its natural, curvaceous course, carved on the steep mountains' valley floor by retracting glaciers. At flood stage, this river (to me) is truly frightening. But where it gouges through our forty acres, not one square inch of it is mapped out as a floodplain. The roaring torrent is completely contained between the banks, even if it brims scarily to the breach-point. Crossing it on our hand tram or on our hundred-foot-long footbridge is intimidating and compels me to rethink every tram anchor and every bridge weld . . . if either ever fails, certain death.

However, there are also two unnamed creeks coming down from the prominent mountain the homestead sits on. Both are big enough to require culverts, but the larger one has washed out the main road to our new cabin at the top of the hill, two years in a row. Both streams ran since the beginning of time with no restrictions, until I showed up. I scratched and clawed up and over a near vertical rock cliff and (miraculously) accessed the upper half of our forty acres. Now I needed to put in a culvert at the bottom of the cliff to accommodate the stream that would otherwise flow down the new road.

The rules of culverts are pretty simple: Make sure the culvert is big enough to handle the stream volume, add about two feet of dirt cover, and have two feet of exposed culvert ends when completed. Check, check, check—done. But a thirty-degree-below-zero cold snap bit down hard and froze the water in the culvert solid. Top to bottom, end to end, solid ice. There was also four feet of snow covering everything, so I had no idea the culvert was frozen shut. Until March. I was walking home on the trail to the cabin and thought I heard water running under the snow—um, not possible. Much like the cowboy getting down on the ground with his ear on the railroad track listening for the ever faint, distant whisper of an oncoming train, I found myself getting down on the packed winter foot trail, ear pressed to the ground listening for the train, and I heard water! "She'll be comin' 'round the mountain when she comes . . ." Water was running under four feet of snow, one hundred feet to the left of the creek, and none in the creek.

This was a colossal problem, and the most likely culprit was the culvert. I shoveled through four or five feet of snow and discovered the culvert was indeed frozen solid and that the water had chosen the ol' "path of least resistance" that ran across our newly developed road and footpath to our home. With a long winter's blanket of snow measuring at least four feet deep, I waited helplessly for the snow to melt, knowing that those faint tricklings I had heard under the snow would increase in sound and volume, eroding everything in their path, including our path. A couple weeks later, I awoke to a new sound. A gushing stream? Hmm. I looked out the window and thar' she blowed—the entire, redirected, fully melted torrent of a stream, running roughshod where it wanted, gouging and rutting what was once a completely landscaped portion of the homestead.

There was nothing that I could do about it except wait for spring. Come April, the ice had melted in the culvert, allowing the stream to return to its natural flow. But as more and more snow melted across the forty acres, you could see more and more damage left behind from the stream that had "jumped the tracks." There were ruts four feet wide by six feet deep—significant damage. One year later, something similar happened to the same stream and culvert. The stream completely washed away the road. I'm guessing about fifty yards (five dump-truck loads) of dirt and rock were washed downstream, leaving a twenty-foot-long culvert with no water running through it. This time around, I upgraded from a 24"-diameter to a 36"-diameter culvert and repositioned it at an angle more accommodating to the stream's flow. I also added ten extra feet to the twenty-foot main section. As we "fall" into winter here in Alaska, I won't know until spring if this fix is going to work. Talk to me in April. Told you. I make mistakes.

SIX

FOREST FIRES AND AIR QUALITY

FOREST FIRES: ALASKA

Alaska is a land of extremes, and forty large forest fires per year raze the forested wilderness. On June 2, 1996, I took off from Talkeetna in a Cessna 185 ski plane headed for Denali base camp. My old friend and mountain pilot David Lee pointed south to a fresh plume of smoke that seemed to have just started. We turned the plane north to Denali, and I never gave it a second glance or thought. Twenty-one days later, after guiding an expedition of eight clients to the top of North America's highest point (20,320 feet) and back, Dave picked me up at the base camp and said, "Remember all that smoke?" It turns out we saw the beginning of what would be called the Miller's Reach fire, which burned 33,000 acres and 344 structures and caused more than ten million dollars of damage—right here in my little Alaskan valley. On the mountain, I had no contact with the outside world (deliberately), and I was shocked to hear many people I knew personally had lost their cabin or home, many without insurance. The number of forest fires per year in Alaska has doubled since the mid-1990s, and if you live in one of the other forty-nine states, pay attention: You're not out of the (fiery) woods yet.

WHY FORESTS BURN

In the last twenty years, the number of forest fires and the billions of dollars of charred devastation left in their wake has increased alarmingly. Ask anyone in the western United States. This region is experiencing consistently hotter temperatures, drier forests, and more droughts, culminating in longer summer-like conditions that extend the fire season. These fires are dangerous for the obvious reasons: They may burn your home to the ground. And for less obvious reasons: They fill the air with particulate matter full of pollutants, like carcinogenic chemicals that are so small they can enter your bloodstream through the lungs, potentially triggering heart and lung problems. Worse: These fires are going global. As I write, Turkey and Greece are battling unprecedented fires, and Australia is still recovering from a fire that killed or harmed a shocking three *billion* wild animals. Fire is going to be in our future, no matter where we live. Even if you settle safely in the "green zone" to the east of the 100th Meridian, you'll be dealing with smoke and particulate matter from western fires.

Wildfires need three elements—a "fire triangle"—to spark: fuel, oxygen, and a heat source. Four out of five fires are started by humans (lightning is the next most common spark). New suburban-style developments in previously wild areas dramatically increase the odds of a fire by bringing combustible materials and people together in close proximity (these are called wildlife-urban interface, or WUI, areas). In 2017, the Tubbs fire in California completely incinerated the suburb of Coffey Park, burning almost 1,300 homes to the ground. As of now, the suburb has been almost completely rebuilt (without fireproof roofing in many cases).

California alone has millions of people living in what the California Department of Forestry and Fire Protection (CAL FIRE) calls "very high fire hazard severity zones." That's millions of people who no doubt love their land, love their homes, and aren't planning on moving anytime soon—despite living on land that is vulnerable to catastrophic fires. Yet, in all of these massive fires, there were homes that survived more or less unscathed. From this we can take an important lesson: It's possible to live, and live reasonably safely, in a fire-prone area. But it takes some thought, time, and effort. In California, any home in a fire-prone area built after 2008 is required to follow a standard—the 7A code—that includes fire-resistant roofs and siding, among other items. Fifty-one percent of homes built to this standard survived the Camp Fire, while only 18 percent of homes built before 2008 did. And why are we focusing on California? I'll give you 39,656,838 reasons (the population of California). If anyone knows what to do right or wrong when it comes to forest fires, it's a Californian.

Californian or not, you have three opportunities to fireproof *your* home. One is in the build, and we'll go through a list of five decisions you can make now that will protect your house from fire for years to come. The second opportunity is in how you prepare the land around your house. The third is in preparing yourself and your family for an emergency evacuation. If you build a house that is naturally fire resilient, and can keep the fire at least one hundred feet away from your house, *and* have a plan for what to do if the fire gets too close for comfort, your odds of surviving an inferno just got dramatically better.

THE FIREPROOF HOME

Many newbie homesteaders and home builders don't understand that flames are not the most dangerous part of the fire. You can avoid the flames: Forest fires can be spotted from many miles away by their classic gray, smoky plume rising into the air. When you see that smoke too close for comfort, you know it's time to batten down the hatches, turn your sprinklers on, and—if possible and advisable—load up your animals, and run.

But what you *can't* see from afar are millions of (deadly) small, red-hot leaves, pine needles, and assorted twigs billowing up with the smoke and creating a fiery "snow" storm ahead of the fire's burn. Winds can carry the (still glowing) flakes up to twenty-five miles, "spotting" the unsuspecting forest with even more new fires miles away. This is known as an ember shower, and many a large structure has been reduced to a billion ashes by just *one ember*. It's surreal to see a home burned down surrounded by green trees. A snowstorm of fiery small embers can spindrift (spray fueled by wind) their way into small crevices, such as gaps between siding boards, or perhaps blow under a house/cabin/trailer should it not have a traditional concrete foundation.

You can see the unpredictable power of a solitary ember when you look at suburban burn areas like Coffey Park in Santa Rosa. Among the devastation are homes that have survived intact. Luck? Maybe. But more likely it is luck plus a homeowner who understood the importance of hardening their house against embers. This can be as simple as screening off attic vents—the most common source of ember ignition in houses.

Now, there's a bigger question about the wisdom of rebuilding in a place that has already catastrophically burned once. Sure, you can take out fire insurance again on a rebuild (at least for now—insurance may be harder to come by as these fires become more frequent). Smarter, though, is putting up a house so resilient to fire that it has fire insurance *built into it*.

The very first thing to consider when you are building your home is ironically the last thing you will actually set in place: the roof and exterior cladding materials. The choices you make here may save—or doom—your structures. If you only have the budget for one big item in your home build, make it your roof. Here's why.

METAL ROOF

A few years back we helped some homesteaders who had what they called a "hobby farm" deep in the Oregon forest. Their forested lot was surrounded by burn scars from a massive fire that roared through their valley a few years previously. Almost miraculously, they were spared.

There was a lot to do, but toward the end of our visit, husband and father Jerry expressed concerns about his leaking roof. I grabbed a ladder, walked around the roof a bit, and realized it was definitely leaking, but perhaps more concerning, this roof was a firetrap. It had an older type of shingle, with some type of paper under it. I'd never seen a roof this flammable, and I shared that news with Jerry as I climbed down. Jerry had had some recent health problems, and I didn't see that leak getting fixed anytime soon. I decided to stop the leak *and* save the house from burning down should another fire pass through.

We tore off the old roof: I still can't believe how flammable those weathered, deteriorated materials were. Imagine old, heavily tarred shingles, with a brown-stained paper product underneath, and you'll understand my dilemma. This homestead dream was one small ember away from going up in smoke. Anyone putting a roof on in the twenty-first century will be using Class A roofing materials, meaning, a roof that is fire-resistant: concrete, clay tiles, fiberglass asphalt shingles, or metal roofing. When I'm replacing a roof in forest fire country I almost exclusively opt for metal. I could rant for pages about different roofing materials, Class A, Class B, and Class C ratings, the pros and cons, etc., but I won't. Why? Most of it's over your head . . . kidding.

But I will share six reasons why everything I own has a metal roof:

1. **FIREPROOF:** I feel it's the most fireproof roof, and firefighters have told me it's a safer roof.

2. **LONGEVITY:** It lasts up to sixty years or more. Most other roofs start to fail at between twenty and twenty-five years.

3. **DURABILITY:** Shingles will blow off in extreme wind while metal will still be clinging to your housetop in 140 mph winds.

4. **INSULATION:** Metal actually keeps your house cooler than shingles. Nonmetal (rubber, asphalt, etc.) absorbs the sun's heat. Your air-conditioning will click on more with any type of asphalt shingle.

5. **AESTHETICS:** I personally think metal roofs look better.

6. **RAIN CATCHMENT:** A metal roof is optimal for collecting rainwater.

A metal roof is one of the biggest, smartest steps you can take as a homeowner to harden your homestead against a fire. Granted, metals eventually will burn, but they require such intense heat (aluminum foil burns at 1,220 degrees Fahrenheit) that you will have bigger problems than your roof catching fire if it ever actually happens!

SIDING

Your next smart move is cladding your house in a fireproof siding. Remember those embers? All these embers need is a crack or gap in the exterior of your house. Once they are blown through that space, and they land on any kind of flammable material—insulation perhaps—you are toast. Screens are your friend. Make sure every gap, vent, or opening is screened. Do you have a clothes dryer? That dryer vent needs a screen. Windows need screens (which will do double duty against insects). Do you have a crawl space? Make sure it is clear of debris and—you guessed it—screened or blocked off and inaccessible to embers.

Here's one homesteading hack for making your own fireproof siding. Cedar, despite being a highly flammable tree, can be treated to be amazingly fire resistant. You can do it chemically *or* literally fight fire with fire by charring the exterior of the wood. Think of wood as a core (lignin) surrounded by cellulose. The exterior cellulose catches fire easily, and burns hot. The interior lignin needs sustained and substantial levels of heat to combust. By charring the wood, you are burning off the exterior—cellulose—layer. The exposed lignin is now much less combustible. If you wanted to burn it, you'd have to build a hot kindling fire, and keep the lignin in it for considerably longer than if you hadn't charred it. Fire resistant *isn't* fireproof. That siding will eventually burn. But it will give you precious time to fight the fire, or make your escape if it comes to that.

Obviously, brick, stone, and stucco are also extremely fire resistant. And cement board, aluminum, and steel siding can resemble wood siding but also serve as fire-protective options for those living in high forest fire regions.

ALTERNATIVE BUILDING MATERIALS

Shipping container homes are literally fireproof. Now, I wouldn't want to be in one during a fire that comes too close for comfort—a toaster oven comes to mind—so you are still going to have to clear your land and establish that firebreak. But, if you are building in a fire-prone area, a house that literally can't catch fire has some *inbuilt* advantages. If you're not interested in living in a metal box but are interested in living in a high fire danger area, consider having a shipping container on your property—again, in a fireproof clearing—as a possible emergency refuge should escape become impossible.

Shipping container/shed roof storage: On homesteads, shipping containers often become barns, storage sheds, and even tiny homes. They are readily available and cost-effective.

FIRE-RESISTANT LAND
PICK YOUR TREES WISELY

I gotta say, I love Idaho. Big mountains, wild rivers, and lots of elbow room for those seeking rurally remote refuge. It also has over twenty-one million acres of pristine, predominantly pine forests that have seen their historical share of devastating forest fires. We've worked on several homesteads in Idaho, two near Sandpoint and one overlooking the very quaint cowboy town of Crouch. All three were surrounded by a burgeoning forest of flammable pine and cedar trees. While we were working in Crouch the temperature reached 106 degrees, making that homestead a tinderbox.

As I worked on these properties I thought about how some trees are more combustible than others. A simple rule of thumb is "Needles burn hotter than leaves." A stand of oak trees is less dangerous than a stand of pine. Why? Two main reasons. Conifers (any tree with needles) tend to be full of flammable sap. They also grow much more tightly packed than deciduous (any trees with leaves) forests. Imagine a pine forest—those trunks are packed in tightly together with lots of low branches that brush up against each other. As the needles fall, they build up a dense mat of highly flammable material. When the forest is finally ignited it burns hot and fast. An oak forest (for instance) is less dense. Each tree has a substantial clear area underneath it. The low-level shrubs, branches, and debris of a pine forest burn quickly, while the oaks burn slowly, not necessarily spreading fire from tree to tree. Not that you have a choice in most of the Western states, where pines are ubiquitous. Oregon's forests, for example, are 86 percent coniferous (the Douglas fir and ponderosa pine being the most common species). Only 12 percent of Oregon's forests are hardwood (another term for deciduous trees).

Trees like the California live oak are uniquely fire resistant, as are mountain ash and beeches. Interestingly, there is one conifer that actively repels fire: the Mediterranean cypress. In 2012, a forestry plantation in Spain burned. All the many varieties of trees were incinerated—except for one stand of the Mediterranean cypress, saved by its ability to store water in its cells. Even the dense mat of fallen needles—usually a fire accelerant—retarded fire by retaining water and creating fewer air pockets within it.

A long-term plan for your homestead might include planting fire-resilient trees around your living area (still not close to the house, but close enough to add visual appeal and give you a shaded area to work or live outside). For the short term, make sure you understand the qualities of the trees that are both on and surround your property. If you live in dense pine, how deep are the needle mats and how thick is the forest? When did it last burn? Even if you can't pick your trees, you can understand the way they behave in a fire, *and* prepare your land to withstand a forest conflagration. Evaluating the forest in this way will give you valuable information about how bad the next fire might be.

Finally, remember that the trees surrounding your property are only one part of the puzzle. You also need to evaluate the trees on either side of your access road, all the way to your closest county, state, or federally maintained road. If there are pines listing over your driveway or road, they need to come down. If there are dense stands of pines or a long stretch of road between you and safety—well, you need an evacuation plan that accounts for the possibility that your road may burn long before your property does (*if* you own the property).

DEFENSIBLE SPACE

Most folks are well aware of their property's potential forest fire danger and of trees that need to be cleared to create a buffer between their respective homes and the would-be flaming trees. Prepping your land to survive an inferno means making hard choices—often about the very things that originally drew you to a property. I remember one Idahoan homesteader who insisted on keeping a half dozen fully grown cedar trees right next to his house. We had finished clearing a significant border around his house, but he was adamant about wanting these trees: "Cedar trees are the least flammable in Idaho." I listened to that in disbelief, then gave my completely opposite two-cent rebuttal. He punched back with, "My neighbor is a forester and I'm taking his professional intel over yours." He said it with such conviction, I second-guessed myself, wondering if he was right.

There was a lot of talk about the "cell structure" of trees and the "natural oils." I'm not inclined to argue with folks that I've come a long way to help, and sometimes it's best to say nothing. But, any card-carrying forester would tell you that cedar trees rank right up there as one of the *most* flammable, and every badge-wearing Boy Scout would tell you that cedar makes the best kindling for starting a fire. And, as irony would have it, a forest fire broke out the next day and the sky turned to smoke. We carefully monitored its direction of burning, as there was only one road down this mountain and no one wanted this escape route closed off by fire. And then, it happened. A forestry truck drove up bearing a card-carrying and badge-wearing forester. He was there to warn us about the encroaching fire, and took the time to commend us for the newly cleared "safe space" around the cabin.

After the greetings, warnings, commendations, and farewells were said, I asked him as he was driving away, "Hey, are cedar trees considered flammable?" He looked at me as if I was kidding and laughed, "Yes, extremely." I was of course kidding, but I really needed that particular guy to say it. I liked this couple and I'm sure they are thriving out there in rural Idaho. But they do live on a one-way dirt logging road and will forever be faced with the threat from forest fires.

––––––––––––––––

It's not just our friends in Idaho. I would say 90 percent of the homesteads we've visited had at least one of the tree species found on my "most flammable trees" list. Cedar, pine, spruce, fir, hemlock, juniper, yew, acacia, and sequoia. These trees are beautiful, breathtaking even, but in a drought- or fire-prone area they can also be deadly.

Be advised, if any of these trees are plentiful and within fifty feet of your home or outbuildings during a forest fire, those structures will most likely burn to the ground. If you seriously want to protect life and property from an encroaching forest fire, you will need to add a new phrase to your vocabulary: defensible space. A defensible space is exactly that—a safe distance between your home and a forest fire. Fires need fuel, and all things flammable (forest) within this buffer zone need to be addressed. Trees, bushes, dry grass, woodpiles, lawn furniture, propane bottles, and even landscaping bark can walk the fire to your front door. What is the recommended distance of a defensible space? One hundred feet. But focus hard on that first fifty-foot distance.

Many cities have ordinances requiring homeowners to mow down tall grass and weeds and control their brush growth. Before the Santa Rosa fire, many Californians and other suburbanites thought clearing dead leaves or dried brush was "a country thing." However, I doubt you'll find complacency now. In 2020 alone, wildfires burned over 4.3 million acres, destroyed 10,500 structures, and killed 31 people. How many of those people didn't have defensible space? I'll never know. But consider yourself enlightened (and warned) and heed these proven steps that you can take to survive a forest fire.

Zone One: Defensible Space

Zone one is the fifty-foot defensible space immediately surrounding your house. This is often the most painful area to address: Beautiful landscaping around a house is often a homesteader's favorite thing about their property. Some very flammable shrubs are commonly found near the house, planted in an aesthetic blanket of tree bark landscaping. But that "beauty bark" burns hot, and juniper, manzanita, acacia, bamboo, chamise, Algerian ivy, and broom are highly flammable shrubs you definitely want at least thirty feet from your house. Make sure your gutters and roof are free from dry branches, pine needles, and fallen leaves. Be mindful of stacking dry firewood up against your house. It's convenient to have your firewood close but not so close that it becomes a catastrophic *inconvenience*. Remnants of lumber and plywood from some long-finished interior house project often end up stacked against the exterior of the house. For years. Each year, getting drier and drier . . . Not good! It's fine to leave some trees and perhaps introduce some landscape shrubbery. But a half dozen trees over sixty feet tall close together could become one united fiery torch and most likely burn your house down. Personally, within the fifty-foot buffer, I would cut five of them down.

Zone Two: Buffer Zone

Once you've created a fifty-foot defensible space around your home in Zone One, think of Zone Two, a one-hundred-foot buffer that allows for some trees, shrubs, stored wood, etc., but with precautions. Trees and shrubs should have (at least) a ten-foot spacing, and trees need their bottom limbs trimmed as high up as you can reach to minimize ground fire from igniting low-lying branches. These low branches are called "ladder fuels," because much like you when climbing a ladder, the fire starts at the bottom of a tree and climbs (burns) its way up to the top, branch after branch, igniting the mass of the tree, creating an inferno. Now it can easily jump from tree to tree, especially when assisted by wind. You can see the wisdom behind tree removal, tree spacing, and tree trimming. All play integral roles in fire prevention and property preservation. But even if you've dotted every "i" and crossed every "tree" when it comes to defensible space, your home is STILL vulnerable to fire from yet another formidable foe, the airborne forest fire ember raining in from the sky. That's where your house-hardening will pay off. If you've cleared all the flammable organic material from outside your home, and made your physical structure fire resilient with screened-off vents and attics, your odds of survival just got exponentially better. Better, but not perfect.

THE ESCAPE DRILL

Sometimes you have no other option than to run. In the last few years, several California towns have been overrun by flames and completely destroyed. Some people made it out, some did not. When you've invested all your savings and all your sweat and love into a property, it's hard to leave. But a wise homesteader understands that in a serious inferno, the fire is going to win. This is doubly true for *homesteading families*. If you have children, clearly their safety comes before your homestead. So the final step in building fire safety into your homestead is developing a plan to run, making sure each member of the homestead understands their role, and drilling it over and over.

We were scheduled to help a family near Redding, California, and I was looking forward to working in this beautiful state. Full disclosure: When I travel far to assist those in need, I'm focused on the work and don't have time to see the sights. However, Redding wasn't far from the redwoods, and it was a lifelong dream of mine to see just one, in person.

But the headlines became awash with news of a firestorm sweeping close to Redding. For thirty-nine days in a row, the Carr Fire burned everything in its path, including 1,100 homes, racking up a whopping 162 million dollars in damages. Sadly, eight lives were lost. The producers monitored the fire and the prospective homesteaders' safety closely, and fortunately their lives and property were spared. Then, as planned, we rolled into Redding and saw the still-smoking aftermath of what came to be called the Carr Fire. Block after block of residential neighborhoods with all the houses burned flat to the ground, and with all the family vehicles still in their garages, or parked in the driveways. Hundreds of vehicles all looking somewhat the same—rusty, brownish, deformed by extreme heat. I noticed the distinct shapes of varying classic cars and trucks. It was eerily apparent this fire caught everyone unaware. Blindsided by the blaze, these unsuspecting folks were lucky to get out with their lives. Nobody was able to save anything. And now they'd all returned to the neighborhood, shuffling carefully through unidentifiable shapes of twisted metal and broken melted glass in search of family albums, heirlooms, or perhaps more realistically . . . anything, *anything*, hidden beneath this sea of ash.

Our homestead destination was an hour's drive from Redding, and every mile went through dry grasses and drier forest stands. Were these California homesteaders prepared for a forest fire? We pulled in and met a beautiful family of five. We immediately saw two things: Number one, these guys were 100 percent legit when it came to farming and animal raising. And number two, these guys were 100 percent "ill-legit" when it came to forest fire preparedness.

The home had dry grass right up to its base, dry bushes rubbing against the house, and dry pine trees in very close proximity (three feet) around the house. Those trees had "rained" down dried pine needles, dead (also dry) branches, and even sap across significant portions of their asphalt-shingle roof (also flammable). The winter rains washed enough of those flammables down to the gutters to actually fill them to the brim. Interestingly, this was one of the smartest (and hardest-working) homesteaders I had ever met. He knew exactly what needed to get done, but when Dad's supporting a large family and building a big homestead simultaneously, his forest fire–prevention plan often moves to the . . . back burner. Don't laugh; every single one of the thirty-nine million California residents should heed the somber life and times of all those who suffered loss in Shasta and Trinity counties.

It was invaluable to stop to talk to the Carr Fire survivors as they stood in the ashes of their life's work. On a charred street, Matt noticed one house had miraculously survived, while the two neighboring houses (in very close proximity) had burned to the ground. Matt learned from the homeowner that he had time to put up some sprinklers, directing the water squarely on the house. It clearly worked, and with Whiskeytown (a town near Redding) still smoldering, Matt began to install a multi-sprinkler head design pointed at the roof and walls of the homesteaders' fairly large home, but also at the grounds approaching the house. We cleaned out the gutters and brought in twenty-first-century, state-of-the-art logging equipment (thanks to Ponsse), which made short work of extensive (considerably large) tree removal, providing a significant, safe, fire-resistant perimeter designed to protect life and property.

While we were preparing this homestead for the next forest fire, one broke out. It was far enough away not to panic, but definitely close enough to monitor. Either way, this house now had a fighting chance against a "firemidable" foe.

FIRE AND LIVESTOCK

But what about the one horse, six goats, and twenty-four rabbits (did I mention chickens)? We now pondered an escape plan for ALL of our four-legged (and beaked) "homesteaders" as well, tapping into a homestead from days of old. We'd call it the Ark. I took a twenty-four-foot-long flatbed tandem axle trailer and at the front built a single-horse stall. Next to that, a separate goat pen. Rabbit hutches were built to accommodate a bunch of bunnies, but there was no room for the chickens. We found an old trailer on a neighbor's property made out of the back half of a pickup truck. We converted that half truck/trailer into a two-wheeled, towable chicken "coupe." Lastly, we installed a towing ball hitch on the back of the twenty-four-foot long Ark. The Ark was deliberately integrated into (parked next to) the goat pen, with the chicken "coupe" nearby.

It was time to test this menagerie, and with not-so-distant fires burning, there was "Noah" time to waste. We gathered the family, grabbed a stopwatch, and ran the family through a good old-fashioned fire drill.

3, 2, 1, GO! The amazing ten-year-old twin girls (they had prizewinning show rabbits) weren't home, so it was down to Dad, Mom, and their number one son (who was seventeen) to simulate a quick, lifesaving exit when faced with a raging forest fire. The boy quickly ran to the fire-prevention sprinkler system, simply throwing a switch and opening some valves, and water immediately strafed the roof and exterior walls of the house, including the ground surrounding the house. "Four minutes!" The trailer served as a home for the goats, so the goat roundup went smoothly. The family worked swiftly as Mom guided Dad (in the trusty family Ford) back toward the Ark, where the hitch was secured and ready to go. "Seven minutes!" Wait—not yet. The chickens!! The family grabbed the tongue of the trailer and (easily) rolled the "coupe" over to the back of the Ark and dropped it into the recently installed towing ball hitch. "Nine minutes!" Now with goats, rabbits, and chickens on board, Dad pulled right up to the horse corral. The loading ramp for the horse was strategically on the side facing the corral gate, and much like a bus driver, Dad pulled up to the horse's stop. Down went the ramps, but no one was sure this persnickety horse would "ride the bus." Yet, as if it figured out everyone else was leaving, and I mean everyone, that horse walked up that ramp like his life depended on it.

Mom secured the door behind her equine prize and jumped into the truck alongside their number one son and . . . Noah. Three connected vehicles (truck, trailer, and "coupe"), all carrying precious cargo, made their way to the paved rural road to safety. "Fourteen minutes! You guys are amazing!"

I've always admired this family. They embrace their self-sufficient lifestyle as a family unit, and the parents travel long distances in support of the twins' mutual dream to breed and show award-winning rabbits across multiple states. I've seen the smiles on their faces, and the award-winning ribbons.

Had we not been significantly impacted by the still-smoldering Carr Fire while traveling to this homestead, we may not have been so focused on the safety of everyone and everything on this property. Had we not talked to those who lost everything they owned, including family pets, had we not talked to those who had a small yet effective sprinkler contingency plan that resulted in saving everything they own, perhaps we wouldn't have installed the same proven system, nor would we have built an Ark. And little did I know, as I was acting as an authority on fire prevention, that my family would later fight the fight of our lives only to lose to a house fire and stand there helplessly, with our fire extinguishers exhausted and our water frozen, watching fifty years in Alaska go up in smoke. I'm living proof—houses burn. Did I rebuild? Yes. Is there a better fire-prevention plan in our new cabin? Definitely. All stoves and chimney pipes are brand-new and a sufficient number of fire extinguishers are throughout the cabin.

SEVEN

BUILDING YOUR HOME

Putting the home into homestead

SHORT-TERM HOUSING

I've rolled up to homesteads with families living in all kinds of buildings, tents, yurts, shipping containers, RVs, school buses, trailers, and cabins. And I've worked with families who've built conventional homes that would fit into a regular suburban setting. Many of our homesteading families have purchased properties that already have living structures on them. Some of these older houses are solid and safe. Many have structural issues, often foundations that are being eroded by water or that were never constructed correctly.

As you plan your initial setup, look for a flat area with some elevation, and not too close to any running water (flash floods are even worse in temporary housing). Do you have a driveway? If not, that will be your first move. Nothing will churn up your land into a field of mud faster than bringing cars, pickups, tractors, backhoes, and maybe even excavators

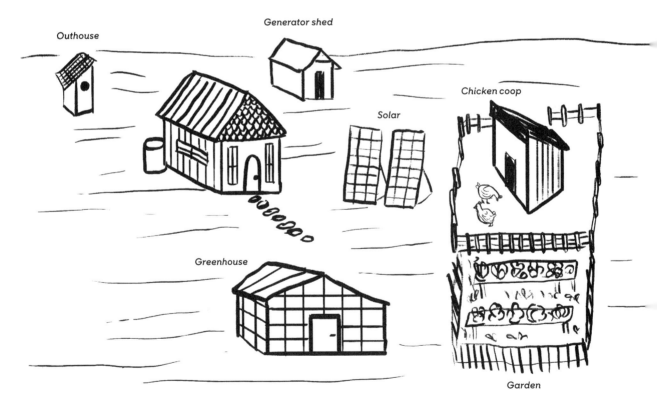

Outhouse

Generator shed

Solar

Chicken coop

Greenhouse

Garden

Homestead layout: Homestead starter kit.

onto it. All rural areas have "that guy" who will clear and level a driveway for you. But you want "that guy" to engineer a very slight upward curve in the middle of your driveway. This is called crowning, and it will stop water from stagnating and sitting on your driveway after a heavy rain. I can't overemphasize the importance of a stable driveway or road.

If there's no flat ground, you may need to build a basic platform for your initial temporary living structure. You'll also need an outhouse and a showering area (see the outhouses section below).

RVS AND CAMPERS

In the movie *National Lampoon's Christmas Vacation*, Cousin Eddie has fallen on hard times and lost the family homestead. Not to worry! He has a housing plan for his wife and two kids. "Hey, where'd you get the tenement on wheels?" asks a surprised Clark Griswold. "Oh, that there's an RV," boasts eggnog-wielding Cousin Eddie. I'm not sure Clark was overly happy about his new unsightly lawn ornament. Cousin Eddie went on to explain how roomy it was for the family of four and that it had all the modern conveniences. Many of our families move onto the property with a camper or trailer or RV. And as Eddie will attest, this is a great option for a property without an existing home.

If you're going to be living on your property in an RV for months at a time, you'll want an outhouse and a shower house of some kind, to avoid having to deal with emptying the tanks of gray or black water. Alternatively, if you have some kind of septic system on the property, you can hook up to it.

If you're willing to drive off-site semi-regularly, there are plenty of gas stations that have both a dump site (a place to empty your sewage) and a place to fill your water tanks with potable water. You do have another option (the one that Cousin Eddie prefers), and that is to empty your raw sewage into the storm drains found on the sides of every road in America; however, if we've learned *anything* from Eddie it's this: If you choose to empty your sewage into a storm drain, it's a bad time to light a cigar. And, if you ever hear "-----er's full, Clark!" Run!

Remember that campers have significantly less insulation than a cabin or house. They have pipes that can freeze and burst, and electronics that might not work well in deep cold. You'll be using a significant amount of propane to run the furnace (trying to heat the cabin with a heat pump system during winter will risk burning it out). You'll want to figure out some way to insulate the base of your RV (with an RV skirt or a DIY solution). There's a reason most RV or camper owners keep them covered, in storage facilities, or otherwise out of the elements when they aren't being used. Sun and rain and snow will do a number on your RV. If the interior gets wet, you may very quickly have a black mold problem (which put our homestead mom in Louisiana in the hospital)—something that is hard enough to fix in a house, let alone an RV.

Finally, old campers that are towed onto a property as a "temporary" living solution tend to become "permanent" eyesores. Unoccupied campers that aren't being heated and aired out on a regular basis will literally start to rot away and quickly become unusable. The more dilapidated they get (like Eddie's), the harder they are to move. We've seen old campers that need to be torn apart by excavators because they are too unstable to tow away. Yet for most homesteaders there aren't enough hours in the day to figure out how to get rid of them—especially when their tires go flat and they stop being roadworthy. Worse, these old semi-abandoned campers can quickly start to look like home for snakes, rodents, and other homestead friends that you don't want to encourage to get too neighborly. And believe it or not, we've showed up on a homestead where the homesteaders were living in two rickety campers where rattlesnakes literally were getting inside through small, round holes.

When that old camper has reached the point of being unusable, don't forget to reduce, reuse, recycle. Old trailers can be stripped down to their metal beds and axles and repurposed as utility vehicles or even the trailer bed for a tiny house. In Season Eight, Matt transformed an old pop-out camper into a junk trailer by utilizing the trailer bed frame. (I've used some of these old trailer frames as bridges to cross small streams.) You won't be saving any wood or laminates, so you don't need to worry about black mold, and you can save a good chunk of change on a trailer bed purchase for a tiny home build.

Even if you are going the frugal route, you can still have fun. Since we were filming right down the road from Elvis Presley's old stomping grounds (Tupelo, Mississippi), I carved an eight-foot-long sign from Matt's trash hauler that read RETURN TO CINDER. Next, I carved a ten-foot sign to go over Misty's garden gate reading ELVIS PARSLEY. We built the family a goat barn that looked exactly like Elvis's childhood home. That twelve-foot-long sign read: HEARTBREAK GOATEL. And last, the new dog house sign read: YOU AIN'T NOTHIN' BUT A . . . HOUND DOG. And, since you're putting down new roots, why not put up new signs? Give that homestead, the road to it, the meadow you drive by, and the creek you drive over a name. We call our forty-acre homestead "Raney Ranch," and the road to it, the "Cliffs of Insanity."

WALL TENT

Another temporary living solution is a tent. Now, there are two kinds of tents. The first is your classic camping tent: small, packable, lightweight. The second is a structured wall tent: room-size, with a high ceiling, a stovepipe vent, and space for a full-size bed, table, and small kitchen area. Some tents can be expanded with "mud room" style vestibules, which allow you to keep the tent clean and organized. Living in the first kind of tent for months at a time? That's a no-go! Sure, it can be—and has been—done by homesteaders with no other options, but if you are living in cramped discomfort for months at a time, your enthusiasm and energy for the hard work of homesteading are not going to last long (and remember, some areas don't allow long-term tent camping, even if you own the land). A well-made wall tent, on the other hand, can be warm, comfortable, "homey," and generally a good place to live.

Look for a tent with all the "extras": windows, that stove and stove vent, bug screens, substantial and well-treated canvas. This will set you back a couple of thousand dollars *but* it will earn its keep. We use a wall tent for hunting trips, or as a shelter for working on projects that need to be protected from the rain or cold. Once you have finished your build, be it a log

Wall tent setup.

cabin or small structure, the wall tent can be packed away or even resold (though personally I'd hold on to it; just make sure to pack it well and keep it free from mildew or mold—every so often take it out, unfold it, and air it out in the sun). Caveat: Even though I like wall tents, it's rough living, and not to most people's tastes. If you are bringing kids, or a spouse who's not interested in "roughing it," this isn't the option for you.

SCHOOL BUS

A school bus, once you've pulled out the interior seats, is essentially a blank slate. You can build it out in a way that makes sense for you and your family. There's no wasted space with a bathroom and no moldering cupboards or fridges to deal with. If the bus is nonoperational and staying put, you can add a small second floor or observation deck by cutting through the roof (just be careful to add bracing to maintain the structural integrity). If you can find a bus that runs, and you have basic mechanical knowledge (and the ability to keep the tires inflated on your homestead), you can keep it roadworthy and it will offer a solution to our forest fire and flood dilemmas in the previous chapters (our Hawaii family from Chapter Three is now equipped with a running school bus/home primed and ready to run from another lava flow). Easier to find are small transit buses (think retired tourist buses or airport shuttles). Again, I don't see these as long-term homes. But they can serve as a great *first* home on a homestead.

Anyone wanting to homestead in Hawaii should reach out to transit companies, as they have to pay significant money to ship used or broken buses back to the mainland. You may end up finding a temporary homestead dwelling (bus) for under five hundred dollars.

IN-TOWN RENTAL

Finally, it's feasible to live off your property and develop it slowly. Here's the deal though: The more time you spend off the property, the slower your progress in developing the property. Your budget will be diluted between maintaining your town life and your homestead life. For a lot of people this is just how it has to be, but if it is an option, consider living fully in town for another period of time to save up the cash to commit fully to your home.

YURTOPIA

My son Miles and his girlfriend live on the upper twenty acres of our homestead in a yurt, year-round, in harsh Alaska. The yurt—a circular dwelling, made of a wooden frame hung with heavy canvas and often topped with a skylight—originated in Central Asia thousands of years ago.

Now, here's my one hesitation about yurts. Despite the many charming pictures of them sitting in remote snowy fields, yurts can be *cold*. Traditionally the floors are covered with felted wool rugs. The walls rely on heavy canvas to keep in the warmth, with minimal insulation opportunities (yurt insulation is generally a variation on foil-lined bubble wrap that sits between layers of canvas). While it is possible to insulate the walls and crank up your wood-fired stove, below 20 degrees Fahrenheit yurt dwellers are in a losing battle to keep warm. The biggest problem is insulating the flooring.

In more temperate climates, yurts can be a great option for a small family. The circular shape makes them resilient to wind storms (the wind flows around the curves of the building, putting less pressure on the structure than it does on flat walls), and their unique structure, with multiple points of connection in the wood frame, makes them flexible in the event of extreme weather or earthquakes. Families can build bunk beds and lofts, and get creative with interior walls to add some privacy and make the large open space more workable.

Despite their nomadic origins, only a die-hard yurt owner would claim that modern yurt living is still truly nomadic living. In truth, I have yet to see a yurt owner move his yurt. My son's yurt is on a permanent wood foundation. And in the story you're about to read, I built a yurt on a massive forty-thousand-pound concrete slab. "Yurt" might want to buy a couple extra yaks if you decide to move this home. In Tennessee we worked with a family of seven who were living in a bus, with the oldest daughter sleeping in her car, two younger boys sleeping on the bus, and two older boys sleeping in the community cook shack. Despite having to haul water and share one outhouse, this family was filled with homesteading joy and love for their property and land. Still, we saw some ways that their lives could be drastically improved.

As it turned out, we had been contacted by the owners of a yurt company who said they wanted to help us if ever there was a need, and this was it. Calls were made, deals were done, and the owners of the yurt company delivered the thirty-foot-diameter yurt from Michigan to Tennessee, free of charge. However, I was also faced with the (COVID-driven) 300 percent lumber price increase. Since yurts need a significant amount of treated posts and joists, and plywood to set the platform on . . . cha-ching. Off the top of my head I figured up to five thousand dollars for all the materials, at least.

Here's where a yurt really shines: Tennessee has cold winters, but not severely cold. An insulated yurt would provide year-round housing with a small footprint that would dramatically improve their quality of life. Not that the family knew anything about it. I told the family I wanted to clear some trees out to make room for parking (important when you are living in a collection of vehicles), to which they were amenable. However, my real motive was to create a fifty-foot-diameter circle to pour a thirty-foot-diameter foundation for their future home. As always, I was working against the clock, so we cleared the area and made a solid, flat gravel pad in half a day.

That night, we brought the family over and asked them to each stand where a truck or car could park. They were milling around their new, respective parking spots when I said to dear ol' Dad, "Wait, you can't park there!" He looked confused . . . asking, "Why not?" I replied, "Well, Dad, you're actually standing in your new living room!" And now with the entire family looking at me confused, I let the "yurt" out of the bag. "We're going to build you a shelter, it's going to be round, and that's all I can say about it." Interestingly, our families *never* guess correctly when we have something big planned for them. This family was no exception.

I decided to pour a thirty-foot-diameter, four-inch-thick concrete slab to set the yurt on. The concrete cost twelve hundred dollars, and I think the concrete company donated most of the mud (cement), leaving us with a huge savings to put somewhere else. Now, Tennessee has semi-mild winters and minimal frost, so I decided to install in-floor heat. The team tied 3/4" PEX tubing to the wire mesh (the wire in a slab to keep it together in case it cracks after being poured) and stubbed out the two ends where you would put a boiler or a hot water heater. Then we put a circulating pump in line with the heat source and boom, filled the system (the tubing in the slab) with nonfreezing fluids (in this case, glycol). This fluid is heated with the boiler or hot water heater, and the circulating pump moves the heated water through the slab. The thermal mass of the concrete (often poured on top of 2" blue board for better heat capture/radiance/performance) absorbs the heat and serves as a thermal battery, and this slab is now nearly fifty thousand pounds of heated concrete to meet and greet their feet all winter long.

While I worked on this project, Matt helped the boys build a workshop, and Misty worked on a solar-powered aeration system (to oxygenate a stagnant pond).

Two days later we knocked on the door of the bus and had the family meet us on the slab. We lined up the family on the beautiful, smooth, hard-surfaced concrete slab and asked them what they thought I was up to. Before they could answer, I whistled and the yurt company owners pulled up, towing an enclosed long tandem-axle trailer with a yurt logo on the side. They jumped out of the truck, and I introduced them to all the family members.

As the owners of the company revealed what was in the trailer, an overwhelming reality set in; tears of shock, appreciation, and disbelief began to flow as each family member was trying to absorb what this meant to them personally. Privacy. Space. Comfort. Cleanliness. Independence. Pride. Everyone was in tears. Yurtopia.

We revealed that we were putting in a septic system, an indoor flushing toilet, a loft in the yurt, doors, windows, a skylight, hot water, a bathtub, a kitchen, and a woodstove. The hits kept comin', and so did the tears. We found and tested an old overgrown well on the property that actually had good water and enough of it to run the homestead. Before we left, this family had gone from living in vehicles to having all the basic, modern household amenities. When we asked the teenage boys if they'd like us to rip out all the community kitchen stuff in the storage building and convert it into a cabin, a cabin they could call their own, emotion overcame them, especially the younger one.

This particular rescue was made even more special by a very unexpected guest, Jackie Siegel, a.k.a. the Queen of Versailles, who is famous for building the biggest home in America (as seen in the documentary that bears her nickname). It turned out the homestead mom worked for one of Jackie's businesses, and when Jackie got wind of their needs, she decided to pitch in. Jackie gifted this family with a complete kitchen and furniture for the entire yurt. Not only that, she brought four suitcases of winter clothes—enough to keep the entire family warm and clothed throughout the Tennessee cold (a total value of well over ten thousand dollars).

The biggest home in America helped us build one of the smaller homes in America, but one thing's for sure: Everyone from the Queen of Versailles to the Pawn of Palmer (Palmer, Alaska, a.k.a. my mailing address) understood that the first word in homestead is *home*, and that this deserving family of seven needed a *home* on their homestead.

Be it bus, or storage shed, or yurt. Be it ever so humble, there's no place like . . . dome.

OUTHOUSES AND SHOWER HOUSES

No matter what your living situation, you will need a rudimentary bathroom. In a more conventional build, that's a simple issue: Plumb in a bathroom, and add a septic. However, most homesteaders need a cheaper, faster, and easier solution.

Very early on in *Homestead Rescue*, we worked with a couple who had never built an outhouse. They were relieving themselves in the areas surrounding their small living structure. Good sanitation is nonnegotiable. These homesteaders were also raising hogs, who were free range and foraging for food. You do the math on what they might have been ingesting along with the acorns and grubs. Their living structure was small and had no room for indoor plumbing, but we were able to build them a bathhouse, with a toilet and a hand-carved wooden tub made out of a mighty oak that we felled on their property. Another couple was using a five-gallon bucket, situated in the entryway of their small dwelling, without any privacy or amenities. Technically this was a functional solution, but realistically it was tearing the family apart, as it was unpleasant and depressing to use and to see.

This brings up an important point about homestead plumbing, and I'm aiming this point specifically at the men reading this book. If you are lucky enough to have a wife or girlfriend who is willing to homestead, then the *very least you can do* is build and maintain an indoor, flushing toilet in a comfortable bathroom for her. I know plenty of women who say they are fine with using a composting toilet or outhouse, and maybe they are, at least in the short term. But I've met many more families where a bad bathroom situation was causing arguments and resentment, and ultimately leading to people leaving the homestead for more comfortable surroundings. Often, the person who is more excited to homestead relishes the challenges of "frontier living" and views a (very) rudimentary outhouse as part of that. To which I say, "Why?" Mollee and I started out living very simply, cooking on a woodstove and living with almost no comforts or conveniences. As soon as I could I upgraded everything, and now although we live off-grid in Alaska, our two-story log home has a full bathroom on each level. In the long term, warm, clean, efficient indoor plumbing will move mountains in terms of homestead happiness. Homesteading is hard, dirty work and providing this one comfort can make you feel like a king or queen. You may well have to start simple and basic, but as *soon* as you can, upgrade your bathroom facilities. Some homesteaders reserve buckets for solids, and "outside" for urine. Remember that men have an easier time peeing in the woods than women, so expecting your girlfriend, wife, or daughters to disappear off into the brush every time they have to go is simply disrespectful.

The family using that five-gallon bucket? We built them a small bathhouse, centrally located between the few small cabins on the property (each with a few people living in it), with a flushing toilet, a bath, and a septic system. Here's another romantic homestead myth: Many people assume they should have a living structure and bathhouse separate from each other. I disagree: Generally I prefer to install bathrooms inside the cabin or living structure, because they are simpler to heat and light, and it's altogether more pleasant and comfortable to have your facilities close at hand. In this case, however, having a centralized bathhouse made it more convenient for a homestead community spread out over multiple cabins.

Having indoor plumbing is not only good for your relationship, it is good for your health. Human feces can contain parasites and microbes that live outside of the body for months. The virus that causes gastroenteritis is infectious for up to two months. Cryptosporidium—a parasite—can survive six months outside of the body. Tapeworms can travel short distances through the soil. It's crucial to isolate these viruses and parasites and keep them away from livestock and other humans.

Not having running water doesn't disqualify you from having indoor plumbing. It's perfectly acceptable to keep water in a bucket by the toilet and use that to flush. We did this for our family in the lava fields of Hawaii. They now have a septic system, even though they don't have running water. One final point: If you are living in the western states, water needs to be at the top of your mind, always. Even the most efficient toilet is still using 1.2 gallons of water a flush. Multiply that by a few visits to the toilet a day, and by the number of people in your house, and you have a major expenditure of water that would be better spent on *water into your body* than *water out of it*. So make sure that this is part of your calculations when you are considering a property and tabulating just how much water you need to run it.

OUTHOUSE

So this cowboy goes out to the outhouse and, looking down in the hole, sees an old-timer. He asks the fella how long he has been down there. The old man replies, "Many moons, my son, many moons." Since the beginning of time, mankind's number one problem has been number two, and the number one most popular (homestead) solution for the number two problem is . . . the outhouse. Fourscore and many moons ago, our forefathers used . . . the outhouse. Yep, even the White House had a row of outhouses out back that most likely were dug by hand, about three feet by three feet by five feet deep. In the twenty-first century many homesteaders use this same crude yet effective system to manage human waste.

Anyone who camps, hikes, hunts, mountain climbs, or lives off-grid can attest that it takes some effort to maintain cleanliness where there is no indoor plumbing. Still, it's "dooable." Ashes from your woodstove will neutralize those unpleasant odors, as will wood chips or sawdust from the wood lot. Lime also works well, but is not the best when it comes to decomposing the waste. Whatever you're pooping in and wherever you're "dooing" it (either indoor or outdoor) can be made 100 percent odor- and insect-free by sprinkling one of these products on it after every use. In fact, an outhouse can be quite sanitary. Fresh white paint, a traditional toilet seat, a few truck-stop air freshener trees, a can of air freshener, and, of course, some reading material will elevate the experience. (I'd consider it an honor if this book ever graced the shelf of an outhouse, and it does have those two hundred pages...) Anyone in seriously cold climates should try a 2" thick piece of blue board insulation as the top of your outhouse "seat." It's incredibly comfortable and, believe it or not, it actually feels warm the second you sit down on it, even at 30 below zero.

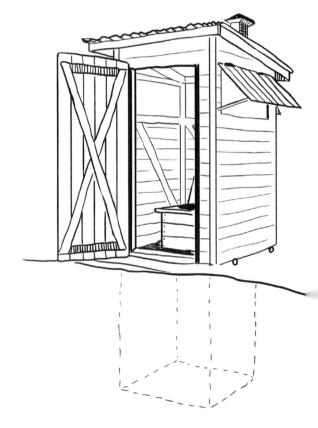

Outhouses are legal in most areas, with some caveats. In Alaska, for instance, an outhouse needs four feet of vertical separation between the bottom of the pit and groundwater, and varying degrees of separation from tidal zones, soil absorption fields, swamps or wetlands, etc. Indiana requires you to connect to the sewer system if it is within a "reasonable distance." In Florida, outhouses are only allowed in remote locations without electrical service, and are specifically banned at permanent residences.

If you do decide to "go" the outhouse route, and you're clear on the rules and regulations for your area, you need to make sure your land is

Outhouse diagram: The number one thing that a homestead needs is an outhouse. The number two thing that a homestead needs is ... an outhouse.

suited to building one. Here's your number one requirement for a functional outhouse: soil with good drainage. If you've ever experienced an outhouse built in clay or on shallow bedrock . . . well, you'll understand why. Outhouses work by allowing the contents to slowly leach into the surrounding soil. Clay or bedrock can form a natural pond. Very soon—after your first big rain perhaps—you'll have a toxic pond. So, as you scout around for where to put your outhouse, think about the soil. You'll be digging a hole roughly five feet deep. Ideally, you want a sand or gravel layer to encourage drainage and percolation. (Don't get tired and quit digging at four feet; you'll regret it . . .)

Line the front of the "box" with clear roofing plastic to shield the wood from urine. It will last longer and smell better.

There are plenty of plans for outhouses online. However, if your outhouse ends up being your permanent bathroom solution, you may want to spend time building something with a bit more space and amenities.

COMPOST TOILET BUILD

A composting toilet is expensive to buy, but possible to build and maintain. At its very simplest, it can be a lidded box with a "seat" over a five-gallon bucket. The bucket is sometimes lined with a compostable liner to make it easier to empty. After each visit, the user sprinkles a good layer of sawdust, coconut fiber, or peat over the latest "deposit." (A heavier layer of organic material is used to soak up urine.) You want to make sure each deposit is fully covered. You'll know you need to add more sawdust (or other organic material) if your toilet starts to smell—a composting toilet that is in balance and is working as desired should have no smell at all, even if indoors. The key to a working composting toilet is the oxygen-breathing bacteria that break down the feces and turn them into compost. To do this you want to keep the contents of the toilet at the right temperature, 60 to 100 degrees Fahrenheit, and you have to keep them moist but not wet. Commercial toilets often come with a fan and a crank to turn over the contents and allow for oxygenation to take place. Most commercial composting toilets are also built in such a way that the urine is collected separately to avoid it creating bad smells, compromising the bacteria, and impeding the composting process. You can figure out your own homestead hack to do this if you are going the DIY route.

Yes, you will need to empty out the toilet. Depending on how many people are using the DIY toilet, you will probably have to empty the bucket or pull out the compostable liner every two to six days. Bear in mind these liners are designed to break down, so don't leave them for long, unless you are willing to risk a clean-up operation that will truly have you feeling like, well . . . you get it. Add the contents to a compost heap dedicated solely to the toilet (*don't* mingle it with your garden compost), and allow it—and its contents—to break down. A long composting time plus sufficient heat is crucial to make sure that any pathogens are fully destroyed (and frankly, you shouldn't assume that a domestic composting pile can fully sterilize the soil).

Finally, I've met a few homesteaders who anticipated using that compost on their gardens. Like many things in the homesteading community, there are multiple belief systems about how to use this compost, but in this instance, common sense should tell you that you want to keep human waste far, far away from any food source. I've had a few homesteaders tell me (very proudly?) that their *plan* is to spread their composted human waste around the base of their fruit trees. But I've never seen one do it. I'm sure that some people do "doo" it, but if you were to ask any legitimate orchard farmer on Planet Earth, "Hey, what would *you* recommend I put on my fruit trees to make them more productive?" he'd respond, "Well, you could put blood meal, soybean meal, composted chicken manure, cottonseed meal, or feathered meal. All of these are all good, natural, nitrogen sources." It would never enter his mind to suggest human compost; in fact, that's an illegal process in commercial food growing and I, for one, am thankful for that.

There are whole books simply about building and maintaining a composting toilet, so read up on your options, and make sure you have a good grasp of the basic chemistry of a well-working toilet. Again, your nose is a great indicator of whether it's working well, or if you've got a problem.

ELECTRIC TOILET

Next, there is what is colloquially known as the "turd burner." It works by heating the "deposits" and turning them into smoke and ash. I know a family of five who paid twelve hundred dollars for an Incinolet toilet and swear by its efficiency and cleanliness. In fact, the company claims you can save two thousand gallons of water per year per person. Theirs requires 220 volts, but there are also incinerating toilets that run on 110 volts. They require power. You have to take care to use a toilet-bowl liner with each use. But they are a great solution in some circumstances. In Season Eight we worked on a homestead outside of Juneau. Not only was the ground wet and saturated, it sat on a shallow layer of mulchy soil over bedrock. Digging a new outhouse wasn't an option, and the existing outhouse was ... full.

The homestead also had an issue with a picturesque stream that was infected with E. coli. The last thing we wanted to do was add *more* bacteria to the land and water—something that would likely happen with another shallow outhouse. In this case, an electric toilet was a good choice, and worth the investment. Not only are they easy to keep clean and sanitary, but now even Mom was willing to visit. If an electric toilet is in your budget *and* if you are living in an extreme climate (whether very hot, very cold, very wet, or very dry), this may be a good option for you.

THE CRIB

Finally, there is a very Alaska situation. Recently, a small sinkhole formed on a street in Anchorage. Upon further investigation, the road crew saw a wooden structure, almost like a small log cabin, under the road. This is a crib, basically a DIY septic system, and something that homesteaders used regularly in the early days of indoor plumbing (and still use in the wilderness or off-grid properties here in Alaska). A crib looks a lot like a simple mineshaft. To build one, a homesteader first digs a shaft down into the ground (again, a gravel or sand layer is ideal), and then sets logs arranged like Lincoln Logs to keep the walls from caving in. Then you backfill the area around the crib, cap it off with a strong and sturdy lid for safety, and completely bury it, leaving a chimney pipe to allow pump access.

The cavity allows solids to sit in the bottom, but the water can leach out between those logs. I have a property with six cabins, two of which still use cribs that were most likely installed in the early 1980s. I just pumped them for the first time in more than forty years of ownership.

I also have rental cabins that have conventional septic systems, which I've installed myself rather than having a professional come out to do it. The first cabin on our forty-acre homestead has a perfectly installed septic that I built, completely to state code. It still wouldn't get that stamp since an engineer didn't sign off on it, but I have the confidence in my own abilities to accept that trade-off.

If you know the basics of how a septic system works, have construction and engineering skills, and follow the specs carefully, you can install a rudimentary system. Here's the deal: A crib septic system may or may not be permitted where you live. You'll have to investigate the local ordinances and decide what kind of risks you are willing to take.

Second, a DIY septic system means that if you try to sell the property, a bank most likely won't finance the buyers. Instead, you'll have to offer owner financing (not always a bad thing, since you can set the interest rate and negotiate the terms to suit you).

ROCKET STOVE TUB

Although my preference is to have the toilet and the bathing facilities within the living structure, the reality is that many established homesteads have some variation of the bathhouse. This is a small structure with the toilet of your choice plus a simple shower or bath, and a hot water heater of some kind. Keeping both toilet and shower in the same structure simplifies the heating and lighting requirements, and means less traipsing over the homestead to get ready in the morning. If luxuriating in long hot showers is your dream, this isn't the route for you. However . . . there is an option that will allow you to have an occasional long, hot bath.

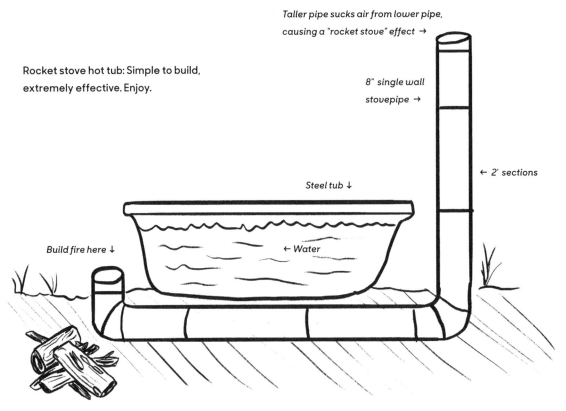

Taller pipe sucks air from lower pipe, causing a "rocket stove" effect →

Rocket stove hot tub: Simple to build, extremely effective. Enjoy.

8" single wall stovepipe →

← 2' sections

Steel tub ↓

Build fire here ↓

← Water

↑ Smaller split wood to fit in 8" pipe

The rocket stove tub is a steel bathtub or a metal stock tank situated outdoors and heated by an open fire, or by a pipe that draws heat from a fire under the tub. The most common rocket stove tubs that I have seen are made with your standard five-foot steel bathtub.

How are you going to heat it? Whereas the simplest method, an open fire pit under the tub, leads to a lot of wasted heat, setting up a rocket stove uses less wood (since all of the heat is concentrated through the stove and pipe) and is more controllable if you want to bring the temperature down quickly without extinguishing the fire (simply block off the oxygen from entering the stove for a few minutes). You are essentially using an eight-foot single wall stovepipe to build a horizontal chimney that runs the length of your tub, does a 90-degree turn, and ends in a stovepipe, at least six feet tall, that safely releases the smoke well over the head of the bather. The hot air rises, sucking in cool air from the other end that is heated over the fire, runs under the tub, and heats the water. And when you light your first fire, it actually sounds like a rocket. You will be shocked by how hot the tub can get. Since 1980, commercial hot tubs have been "maxed out" at 104 degrees, which is hot, but not ridiculously so. Your rocket ship hot tub will get considerably hotter, so bear this in mind and never let children or medically vulnerable people use it unsupervised. Make sure you always have a five-gallon bucket of cold water on hand in case you need to quickly and dramatically lower the temperature.

A hot bath can do wonders for morale on a homestead. Even if you only use it sporadically, having a long soak after a hard, dirty day of work will feel like a true reward for all your efforts on your homestead. Find a spot on your property with a great view, and add a small side table for that cup of coffee. One tip: Build some kind of "bum board" to sit on. The chimney isn't the only thing that needs insulation from the heat . . .

TRASH CONTAINER

You probably haven't given much thought to how you are going to process the trash you generate on your homestead. Why would you? After all, most homesteaders are naturally living the reduce, reuse, and recycle ethos and aren't generating huge quantities of trash. You may have repurposed food and beverage containers to store dry goods. If you buy bottled water or soda, or glass jars full of jams or sauces, those jars and bottles are food-grade glass or plastic. You can repurpose them as kitchen storage for dry goods that you buy in bulk.

Still, you are inevitably going to have a certain amount of items to dispose of on a bi-weekly or monthly basis. The number one requirement for trash storage and disposal is keeping your trash *in* and your neighbors *out*. Plastic bins aren't going to last long once the raccoons or bears have your trash cans in their sights. In a few more chapters we'll talk about bears and how to make your homestead as unappealing to them as possible. For now, think of the bear-proof trash cans and dumpsters you see in state and national parks. You want a substantial metal or wooden bin, with a heavy, lockable lid, and separate cans within it for slops, metals, plastics, and paper. Depending on where you live, you may be able to burn your paper, cardboard, and wood scraps (at least in summer; in winter you should be burning them in your grate to get your stove going). Do your research to make sure that burn barrels are legal in your area. If you are able to burn, do it responsibly.

The overarching goal with your trash is: Keep it to a minimum. Of course, you'll still have recycling, and some refuse is inevitable. But as you develop your homestead, set yourself the goal of finding ways to continually buy fewer conventional items, and repurpose or recycle what single-use glass or plastic you do end up with. Not only is this an environmentally sound reason, but it will cut down on those sometimes onerous trips to the dump, and keep opportunistic foragers at bay.

PERMANENT LIVING STRUCTURES

Once you've gotten your temporary living structure established, it's time to think bigger. All good homestead living structures have a few things in common. They are sturdy enough to withstand bad weather and unexpected floods. They are elevated enough not to be washed away in extreme conditions. They are insulated enough to keep you warm in winter and, ideally, cool in summer. They have well-thought-out interiors that allow you to live life in reasonable amounts of comfort. And they use homestead-approved methods like passive heating and cooling, and solar power to keep your expenditures as low as possible.

So long as your home meets these criteria, the rest is up to you.

In Season Six, we worked with a family who had turned thirty thousand tires into a home. True, they needed a lot of help to refine and finish it (we ended up using an old technique that mixes straw and mud to fill in the thousands of small holes and gaps in their walls). Other homesteaders have built straw-bale houses. One thing—don't rush to move into an existing structure if you don't have some basic building know-how, or at least can assess the structure for potential safety issues. Walls that bulge out, or aren't plumb, are a red flag that your structure isn't stable.

SHIPPING CONTAINERS

Shipping container (also called Conex) homes are not only affordable—around half the cost of a traditional structure—they are robust, sturdy, and look good too. They can—if properly anchored—withstand hurricanes, earthquakes, floods, fires, and pretty much everything else Mother Nature throws at them, other than a meteor. An unanchored box can withstand 175 mph winds. Anchored, 250 mph. The steel box allows the walls to wobble and flex without collapsing in an earthquake. The roof can withstand up to four hundred thousand pounds of evenly distributed weight. There are literally millions of decommissioned boxes—between five and eleven million in the US alone, depending on who you ask. Still, you'll need to do some due diligence to make sure a shipping container will work for you. And remember, every time you cut into the box to add a window or door, you need to account for the way those cuts weaken the structure.

Your first step in building a home out of shipping containers is to go to your local department of housing and development to research the rules for shipping container builds in your immediate area. This can be easier said than done. Because shipping container homes are still relatively novel, you won't necessarily find rules and regulations specifically relating to them. So it will be on you to do some research, make some calls, and ensure your dream home will meet the borough's or county's standards.

Containers come in multiple lengths, from ten feet to forty-five feet. "High cube" containers have an 8'9" interior clearance. Standard containers have an interior clearance a hair under 7'10". So, if you're on the tall—or claustrophobic—side, that's something to consider. Remember that you won't know what was shipped in these containers either. It's possible they were used to ship chemicals or other toxic items (in Los Angeles—and some other counties—you can only use containers that have shipped nontoxic materials). So be sure to clean them thoroughly, and strip away any interior flooring or paneling before you start your build. Keep an eye out for insects, snakes, or other stowaways and make sure to humanely kill them if you find them. You don't want to unwittingly introduce an invasive species to your land.

Your next consideration is to figure out a plan for how many containers you want and whether you have the knowledge and capability to do the build on your own. Two containers in an *L* formation, or three containers in either a *U* or an *H* formation, will work for a small family (one of our families used a *U* formation to build a barn structure for their animals). You'll need a foundation and ideally a pitched roof, so water or snow doesn't pool and promote rusting. If you're adding solar panels, you'll want to orient your house to get maximum sun exposure during the day. Are you adding a bathroom? If so, you'll need to incorporate plumbing and electric into your build.

I'm not kidding when I say that your permanent structure needs to be able to survive bad conditions—something that was reinforced for me on a dusty patch of desert in Nevada, when I jumped into the second part of my rescue for the Kondor family.

A SHIPPING CONTAINER HOME PROVES ITS STRENGTH

The first time I laid eyes (and boots) on a dry, dusty desert was in Lovelock, Nevada. It's so hot there that I saw a coyote chasing a jackrabbit, and they were both walking. The town is named after George Lovelock, who recognized this area as the last stop for water for weary travelers and bought the land and water rights.

When we arrived, the Kondor family's area was in the eighth straight year of a drought. We'd solved their water problems, but now it was time to improve the Kondors' *living* situation. They were only just getting by in several small, single-axle, circa-1970s camp trailers where indoor temperatures reached 100 degrees plus. I placed a thermometer inside to confirm and, whew, confirmation. These guys were way off-grid, so how was I supposed to cool these trailers down? There was no means of power, and no air-conditioning. The only other "building" on the forty acres was a twenty-foot shipping container full of straw bales. Why? They had hundreds of them stacked up as a wind barrier to protect the trailers from the brutal desert winds that carried tons of fine, unhealthy dust, which found its way through every microscopic nook and cranny of the weathered camp trailers. If it wasn't nailed down, it was not going to be there come morning—including the camp trailers. In fact, the three (parents in one, two boys each with their own) trailers were in close proximity to each other, i.e., safety in numbers, and were strategically parked to serve as a wind barrier.

Not so long ago, the original homesteaders passed through Lovelock, Nevada, headed to California. During the 1800s, an estimated 250,000 people ventured west, many headed to California, on a route running through Lovelock. But once you left Lovelock, there was no "Love lost" on the next desolate forty miles.

By 1850, the notoriously infamous "Forty Mile Desert" had become a highway of white, sun-bleached bones and mounded desert grave sites. The documented death toll was 5,000 horses, 3,500 cattle, and 953 would-be Californians. The eighty-seven-member Donner party (irony: when I typed "Donner," spell-check decided "dinner" was more accurate) came through these parts as well, surviving the scorching desert only to succumb to the unusually harsh winter of 1846 in California's Sierra Nevada mountains. I'm sure there was a wooden sign reading LAST WATER FOR NEXT 40 MILES on the edge of town, yet even Mark Twain himself walked by that sign *and* across that very desert. He notably wrote about his experience: "It was a dreary pull and a long and thirsty one, for we had no water. From one extremity of this desert to the other, the road was white with the bones of oxen and horses. It would hardly be an exaggeration to say that we could have walked the forty miles and set our feet on a bone at every step."

Back to the twenty-first century: I decided to empty the shipping container and convert it into a windproof tiny home, piping in cool air through vents cut into the floor. I dug a twenty-foot-long trench, eight feet deep and two feet wide, shored up the trench walls to prevent collapsing, and then centered the 8' by 20' tiny home over the trench. The idea was to take advantage of the cooler desert dirt cavity and use long lengths of 6" buried pipe to create cooled air induction. I put small, low-voltage, solar-powered fans on the inside of the standpipes (the vertical section of pipe sticking up four feet out of the ground) to create air movement, pulling hot desert air and moving it toward the tiny home, to be cooled along the way by the colder air in the trench. Ultimately, it worked.

Next, we installed large windows, a standard 36" front door, a cookstove, and a bath-tub. The mountain vistas, the golden sunrises, and the scarlet sunsets from this forty-acre mountainside were truly amazing. Finally, I built a staircase to the top of this now recon-figured steel shipping container and the 8' by 20' tiny home now had an instant 8' by 20' steel viewing deck.

Has desert living gotten any easier since 1850? Immediately after the doors and windows were installed, the perpetually sunny skies darkened abruptly, and an abnormal, cool breeze swept across the normally hot desert. As I looked down the valley toward Lovelock, a low, thick San Francisco–like fog was rolling toward us. The wind felt pre-tornado-like, and now the weather had everyone's undivided, anxious attention. If it wasn't nailed down, it was airborne. But what was pushing all of this wind? Over the ridge came the answer: a full-"blown" dust storm, descending swiftly upon the forty acres. A clouded, swirling, choking, mountainous mass of dust, dirt, and wind conjured all it could whip up from the desert floor and hurled it at the homestead.

Everyone ran to seek shelter, and now, for the first time ever, these homesteaders had a place of refuge from the desert wind, blazing sun, and their very first dust storm. I made my way through the gale shouting for, and gathering up, Misty and Matt, as well as the homestead mom and two sons, calling to all, "Head for the tiny home, it's the safest place!" As spindrift dust filled the campers through poorly sealed doors and windows, the steel shipping container was undaunted by the desert's dirt and pelting sands. Everyone was coughing and shielding/rubbing their faces and eyes making their way to the tiny home. But Dan (the homestead dad) was missing. I went out to look for him, whistling, yelling, straining to see, but visibility was extremely limited and my shouts were dwarfed by a howling, honest-to-God 1850 dust storm. I went back to the tiny home and thankfully all were present, sans one. I was thinking that the visibility was so bad that Dan was hunkered down somewhere riding out the storm. But right about that (unnerving) time that you really start to worry something bad has happened, out of the dust storm comes the blurred outline of a person, and the door opens and closes quickly behind Dan, carrying his beloved dog. Turns out the dog was lost in the storm, and Dan went to look for him, becoming lost a bit himself. Whew. Riders on the storm . . .

Inside that safe, solid, steel tiny home, we all waited as the menacing meteorological mayhem strafed the notorious Forty Mile Desert. Seven of us (eight counting the dog, which by the way looked *exactly* like Toto) waited safely, surrounded by rigid steel, as the dust storm passed through on its own terms before allowing the Nevada sun to take command once again over clear blue skies. Whew. The skies may have cleared, but it took about a week before my lungs did. The Hollywood-esque dust storm was over. "Move along now folks, nothing to see here." But was there something to learn here, folks? Well, let's see. Deserts are a tough place to homestead. A shipping container proved itself a safe haven during a classic twenty-first-century dust storm. And back in 1850, while every would-be California-bound homesteader couldn't wait to see this desert area of Nevada in their wagons' rearview mirrors, others deliberately chose to stay and put down . . . roots.

As we drove away, the 100-degree temperature was rising, and I swear I saw, in *my* rearview mirror, a fire hydrant chasing a dog that looked a lot like . . . Toto ("paws" for laughter).

LOG HOME STRUCTURES

What's the difference between a log home and a log cabin? Nothing. Although the word *cabin* does connote something quaint, rustic, smaller, and perhaps cheaper, let's not become cemented in semantics. Log structures have been the gold standard for homesteaders since the 1600s. Why? Every homestead most likely had trees of some sort, and trees and logs were a legitimate, readily available building material. I've built my share of log cabins, and currently live in a log home built entirely from dead "beetle kill" trees harvested solely from the property, even though there's a plethora of lumber stores selling dimensional lumber in nearby towns. However, those lumber store prices have increased exponentially, doubling the value of standing homestead trees (perhaps tripling).

Building a home out of logs is easier dreamed than done. Those (now more valuable than ever) trees need to be selected, harvested, moved, peeled, and hand-fitted, requiring specific skill sets beyond those of carpenters and Lincoln Log erectors. It's definitely the most physically demanding home you can build, but in my opinion, nothing says homestead like a log cabin in the woods.

I "wood" say that some type of log home has been built out of every major tree species on earth, but today, the most common tree species used are (certainly not limited to) spruce, pine, cedar, and oak. Many companies prebuild the log home shell, tagging each log end with identification numbers or letters, allowing it to be dismantled and trucked to its new homesite location. Most of the custom log homes you see were most likely hauled there on the back of a truck. I've been involved with restacking at least a dozen big log homes in Alaska that were originally built in Canada, then hauled up the Alaska highway.

> # Nothing says homestead like a log cabin in the woods.

Very few modern-day home-steaders have ever notched a log cabin (the process of cutting out "saddles" or dovetails at the end of each log, to allow them to be stacked). There's a reason for that: You need good logs. Then there's the labor involved. That money—assuming you are paying for materials and some help—stacks up fast. Then there's the fact that log cabins shift, settle, and shrink over time. In my own house I had to come up with a way to build out interior framing that won't shrink, and attach it to log exterior walls that will lose about a quarter of an inch per

Basic one-room cabin: Nothing says homestead more than a log cabin.

log over time (add it up and that's a good few inches in height). I accomplished this by cutting long slits in the frame and attaching bolts through those slits to hold the framing in place. As the cabin settles, the bolts are able to move, maintaining structural integrity.

Nothing would make me happier than to see every homesteader in America living in a handcrafted log home, but it's never going to happen for said reasons. You can still have that log cabin aesthetic in your house, though. Incorporating accent logs into a home is very doable and gives you some satisfaction that your home resourcefully incorporates unique-shaped trees from your property. They can serve as structural beams, bar counters, and tabletops, and if you want to test your skills you can build a staircase and railing. In our house I made a hand-hewn staircase out of a beloved tree that had succumbed to beetles. For the banisters, I sourced heavily burled wood (burls are large knots, caused by either infection or fungus, that cause the wood to grow in dramatic and unusual shapes). But as I've said, I rarely see a homesteader build their own log home out of their own logs. It's hard work.

THERE'S NO PLACE LIKE HOME

We've built several tiny houses on various-size trailer frames. Like the school bus, these have the advantage of being completely customizable and portable. Tiny houses are ideal if you don't actually own the land you are homesteading—as in the case of one couple in the South who ended up having to relocate their home. We helped them build a tiny home on a salvaged trailer bed. Once they landed on a more permanent spot, they added a deck to expand their warm-weather living space.

Here's the amazing thing about a small cabin or tiny home build: You can do it. Get that friend who has carpentry on his résumé. He will keep the structure plumb and square, while you, on a small (tiny) scale, get a big crash course in all phases of construction. This first homestead build can go up surprisingly fast. There's a few reasons for this. One, in a true tiny home or one-room cabin, you aren't going to be digging a basement or pouring a conventional foundation. Instead, you can use a concrete pillar foundation made out of pre-formed concrete pads sold at Home Depot. You can also mix and pour your own concrete pillars on site (we'll go into more detail in a few pages).

Then it is a relatively simple job of framing out the floor, insulating it, putting down a plywood flooring material (and protecting the underside of the floor with rodent-proof wire fencing), and then framing your walls, adding house wrap, cutting out windows and doors, and insulating and finishing the interior. Your hardest job will be the roof, as a danger factor weighs in when working ten to twenty feet off the ground.

For your first simple build, you can do a one-sided "shed" roof with the slope running downward toward the rear of the house (a perfect opportunity for rain catchment). If you want to make a mobile tiny house, you can strip down an old caravan or trailer and frame that out instead.

A 10' by 12' one-room cabin, with a couple of windows and a door, is achievable for one person. If you have some basic skills and can focus exclusively on the build, plan on three to four weeks to get the basic structure in place. A good tip is to make sure that your walls are never too heavy to lift up and install—especially relevant if you are doing the build single-handedly. Before you begin:

- Measure twice, cut once. This old saying is doubly true when you are miles and miles from the nearest lumberyard.

- As you work, use a length of string, a 25' tape measure, a 4' level, and a carpenter's pencil to check for plumb with every step of the install. It's very tempting to force something that is almost correct, but it will throw off your whole build (ever heard of the Leaning Tower of Pisa?). If it's not right, stop what you are doing and figure out a way to correct your error.

- A big part of successful building on homesteads is getting over an understandable fear of chainsaws, table saws, and other fast-moving, sharp-edged tools. At some point you will need to fire up a chainsaw. I use a chainsaw on a daily basis and I highly recommend practicing with it by cutting firewood until you understand how to wield it safely.

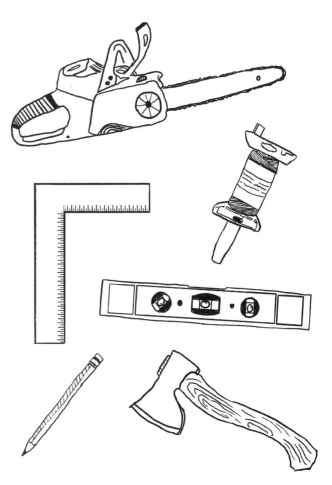

Various tools: With these few tools, you can build a successful homestead. Just add water (i.e., sweat).

- Remember: You're building your home. Every extra step you take to add comfort, stability, and impermeability to your structure will pay off for years down the road.

The Home Build

It seems every guy I've ever met, and half the women I've ever met, have all told me they were . . . carpenters. That's great, because I'm not going to provide floor plans and go into schematic detail on how to build a house from the ground up. I will, however, share some basic, universal info that I hope you find beneficial no matter where or what you choose to build.

Orientation

When you stake out the location of your new home, have the front of your house facing south. Why? The passive (free) heat that your home will absorb through the winter months saves you significant (fuel bill) money. And a south-facing house also allows for maximum natural light from the sun. Bam! Another (electric bill) savings. You'll need to think about how many windows you'll want on that south-facing house front, because those windows will transfer both heat and light. This abundant natural light streaming into your home is actually a health benefit, boosting your immune system. And if you live in snow country, a south-facing home will be less prone to having ice dams build up on the eaves of your roof. OK, good cop, bad cop. If you're building in a much warmer climate, think twice about the amount of windows you design into the build, epecially if you face the home south with the intent to capture more natural light. Come summer, you may be spending more money than needed trying to keep it cool. In fact, you might locate your home near a grove of trees to cool your house with shade (only in a low-fire-risk zone, of course).

Foundations

From gospel singers to motivational speakers, everyone metaphorically sings the praises of the importance of a good, solid foundation—whether it be a marriage, a business venture, or, as in our case, a humble little home.

Here in Alaska, when the ground starts shaking and the dishes start rattling, you'll be wondering how sturdy and well-built your home is, starting with the foundation. This is earthquake country, where virtually every single home has a concrete foundation poured around a grid of steel rebar. And the same can probably be said wherever you live. Concrete is ubiquitous. So, of course, here and now we're going to recommend a concrete foundation to every person reading this. But I know that every person reading this may not have the means ($), logistics (no road access, in my case), or a structure needing a concrete foundation (shipping container), so let's break it down.

Concrete is amazing. I'm in awe of it. I've often said, find me a man who knows all there is to know about concrete and I'll give you a million dollars. It's complex. It's science. It's chemical. It's history. It's evolving. The mortar between the bricks of the 2,240-year-old Great Wall of China is held together with lime and sticky rice. And Roman concrete (volcanic ash and lime) is the reason the Pantheon in Rome is still standing 1,897 years after it was built. Like I said: amazing.

And concrete is cheap. Whether you pour a mono slab, pour stem walls, or lay up a cinder block wall and grout it with concrete, you've just installed the best foundation on . . . earth.

I recommend you find a local concrete man, or two, get some bids and local foundation input. But you can do this entire foundation without a contractor if there's at least one concrete person on the job. He'll keep you out of trouble, yell a little bit, perhaps imbibe, but you'll end up with a square and level foundation ready to build on. A mason takes pride in a job well done. All you need to do is find him. If your concrete slab is done properly, it can also serve as your custom, *finished* floor. The process of staining concrete is quite simple and reasonably affordable. I highly recommend looking into staining your concrete floor.

Treated lumber is a popular foundation-building product, and I've used it myself when building remote structures with no road access, meaning I couldn't get a concrete truck to the site. A short installation version goes like this: Dig a hole past the "frost line" (this hole depth will be in a code book where you live), drop in a minimum post no smaller than 6" by 6" (8" by 8" is better, but . . . $$), surround that 6" by 6" with at least three five-gallon buckets' worth of concrete, and plumb it vertically. Set all your posts on a square layout no farther than ten feet apart. Shoot a level laser line across all the posts, cutting them off evenly. Done. Most likely some angle bracing from post to post will still be required to prevent deck movement (shaking), even after the floor joists and 3/4" plywood are constructed.

Now, how long will that treated post last? Well, the guy selling it to you will say, "It'll last a hundred years!" but that same guy won't be around to back that statement up when it fails at thirty years. Other intel claims that treated posts can deteriorate as soon as twenty years. Clearly it depends on the soils, the moisture, the heat, and even termites. Yep. People claim that determined termites bore their way through (alleged) bug-resistant treated lumber products, compromising a foundation's integrity. I find that to be rare, but it "bugged" me enough to share.

What's better than treated posts as a house foundation? Concrete-filled sonotubes. A sonotube is a hollow tube made out of heavy-duty cardboard. Installation is quite basic: Dig a hole to accommodate your sonotube, drop it in, backfill it in place, and then fill it with concrete. They come in all diameter sizes: 6", 8", 10", and 12", but again, 6" or 8" is more than adequate to build any home on. Dropping in two pieces of 1/2" rebar reinforces its strength, and last, you'll need a post bracket set in the still-wet concrete, allowing you to transition from concrete to wood.

When it comes time to fill the grid of sonotubes with concrete, most people will go to Lowe's or Home Depot and buy bags of premixed concrete (just add water). But anyone wanting to save a little money can mix that concrete in a wheelbarrow, from scratch. And it's as easy as 1, 2, 3. Literally: 1 part cement, 2 parts sand, and 3 parts rock (stone). Use a shovel to equally add each component (one shovelful of cement, etc.). I recommend you dry mix your "full" wheelbarrow, adding the water *after* you feel the cement, sand, and rock are thoroughly (dry) mixed. Do this mix right, and you have just produced 4,500 psi concrete. It will reach that strength twenty-eight days after you pour it (gotta love the science!). You can buy a plastic bell-shaped footer that goes in the bottom of your sonotube hole first, which provides a much more stable "footing" system than just setting your sonotube in a hole. Another simple way to create a footer is to simply pour concrete in the bottom of the sonotube hole, which is most likely a bit bigger than your actual cardboard sonotube. A couple small pieces of rebar in an *X* formation will create a reinforced footing for the smaller sonotube footprint to sit on (you can drop in some old small tires to serve as footing forms for pouring the concrete). Whatever sonotube footing system you choose, your foundation will have a better chance of holding up your house a hundred years from now than any treated wood product.

Our log home in Alaska has neither a treated wood nor a concrete foundation. It's off-grid and a torrential, glacier-fed river separates us from the road system (a concrete truck is not an option). It's also built on sloping terrain, so one side of the cabin is ten feet from the ground (too far for a standard-size sonotube). I had heard that Alyeska Ski Resort in Gird-wood, Alaska, was replacing the towers of its one-chair ski lift, so I managed to get eight 18" by 20' steel ski towers for our cabin build. I pounded them into the ground with the excava-tor, much like a bridge piling, cut them all off at the same level, and welded numerous 3" by 3" angle irons at 45-degree angles to cross brace the ski towers, knowing this cabin would feel a lot of earthquakes in its life. (We've already had a few 3- and 4-point earthquakes, but bigger ones are coming for sure.) There's a lot of expensive steel under that cabin, and if I had to buy it, I most likely would not have gone this route because of the cost. But I salvaged all the steel I could, and it has made for a very strong, very affordable, one-of-a-kind foundation.

Next step: Framing

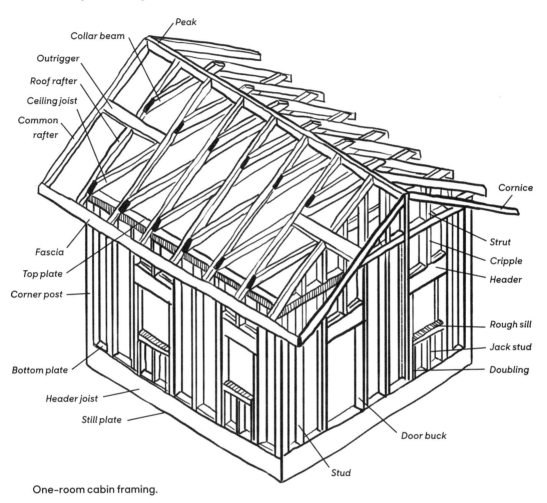

One-room cabin framing.

Once your foundation is in you can begin framing your house. Never go more than 16" on center when laying out your floor joists. (To simplify this, most retractable carpenter's rulers have 16" increments clearly marked. If you own a tape that doesn't have these 16" increments marked out in red, throw the tape away.) Make sure your floor joists are big enough to carry the load you are spanning. And once your joists are down, use a minimum 3/4"-thick tongue and groove plywood as your subfloor. I recommend gluing and screwing it down, that is, if you never want to hear that floor creak. The next step is framing and sheeting your four (or more) outside walls. Again, I recommend all walls, including interior, be framed on 16" centers. It's stronger. Period. And do everything to code, if possible. Building on ski towers may not be to code, nor is a big log home constructed from beetle-killed spruce trees (ours), but if you're working with conventional lumber, there are structural safety reasons why you don't want to cut corners to save money by spacing floors and walls on 24" centers. But once you get to the roof, all trusses and roof rafters are usually spaced out on 24" centers covered by 5/8" plywood sheeting. I'm always going to recommend a metal roof, as it's best for forest fire protection, rain catchment, affordability, and longevity. I was a framing contractor years ago, and we hand-nailed entire houses. But I highly recommend pneumatic nail and staple guns for any of your major framing projects like a home. Can you frame your own house? Absolutely. But again, all you really need is just one true framer on the job to keep you out of trouble. I strongly suggest you consider natural logs in your framing plans, either as a structural or as an aesthetic accent.

Framing goes up fast, and once you install the doors and windows, your building becomes "dried in."

The next step of a house build is roughing in your electrical and plumbing. Most people are going to sub (hire out) this work to "card carrying" professionals. If you feel qualified to do either, then definitely follow the code book. Don't make me say why . . . If you have just one qualified electrician or plumber in your circle of friends to lead the way, wiring and plumbing can easily be done "in house."

Insulation

Once all the basic plumbing and electrical is "roughed in" your walls, it is well within your skill set to insulate your own home (wear a mask). I recommend standard insulated batts that are designed to friction fit snugly between walls built on 16" and 24" centers. Once you've insulated "every square inch," you'll need to check with the codes in your area to see if you need a vapor barrier. A vapor barrier is one layer of clear, 6 mil plastic stapled tightly over every square inch of your insulation. It serves as a "vapor" or water barrier preventing the moisture inside your home from getting into the insulated wall. There's a lot of discussion about whether or not you need a vapor barrier, and it does depend on your climate. I recommend one phone call to a legitimate insulation company in your area. At the end of that phone call you'll be an expert on moisture, barriers, and whether or not 6 mil vapor barriers are required in your area.

Interior Finish

Most builders finish the inside of their homes with sheetrock. Use 1/2"-thick, 4' by 8' sheets on your walls and 5/8"-thick, 4' by 8' sheets on your ceilings. Can you fill the joints and tape those seams, "finishing" the sheetrock so it's ready for paint? Nope. If you've never worked with taping and sanding sheetrocked walls, I doubt you can make it look smooth and professional. This is a true art form, and you'll be staring at those walls and ceiling for a long time. Hey, this is the inside of your home, and if you want to be proud of it, get a pro.

If you're finishing the inside with wood, such as a 1" by 6" tongue and groove, fit those boards as tight as you can before nailing to the framing studs. These boards are going to shrink, and those beautiful pine boards will develop gaps over time. Some boards more than others. If you have the luxury of time on your side, you can buy the product (pine boards) and let them acclimate for a few weeks inside your heated home before you nail them to the walls. This will minimize shrinking joints (gaps) and make for a better-looking finished product.

When it comes to paint and lacquer, there's a million ways to go. I recommend you walk into a bona fide paint store and have a discussion with a professional. This industry is ever-changing and the choices are daunting. Do your own painting? Absolutely.

In conclusion, you'll have plenty of questions before you start any building project, but where will you get the best answers? I recommend talking to LOCAL tradesmen, people actually building in your area. A YouTube video may give advice that won't work in your region—in fact, it may not work in *any* region.

EIGHT

HOMESTEAD TOOLS

What can you build with a Skilsaw (circular saw), a hammer, a drill, a carpenter's pencil, a square, and a string line? Anything on Planet Earth, within reason. But definitely, anything on a homestead. When I think of all the construction projects that I've done in the last fifty years in Alaska, you'd be impressed with how many were done with just the basic tools like the ones mentioned above. Obviously, if you have at your disposal every single tool that DEWALT sells (lucky you), that's a good thing, but it's not necessary.

I see many people building with 3" screws driven by cordless drills. Let me ask you a question. Which makes for a stronger house? One screwed together, or one nailed together? The answer is nailed. In fact, using screws to frame a house and roof system is illegal. Never underestimate the integrity of just one 3.5" nail.

I spent today framing the roof system of a log cabin using only the tools listed above. Clearly, in addition to this list, I am going to recommend a chainsaw.

THE CHAINSAW

Everything you ever wanted to know about chainsaws but were afraid to axe . . .

Any farmer, rancher, homesteader, or weekend warrior (or Hollywood low-budget B-movie horror film actor) worth his or her salt should own at least one chainsaw. In fact, when you pull the trigger on a piece of land (symbolically) the very next trigger you put your finger on (literally) will be a chainsaw. On day one you'll be clearing land, which means you'll be using a chainsaw to cut everything from last year's underbrush to 150-year-old standing trees. The trees will provide firewood to heat your home, as well as provide logs for milling lumber. You will most likely use the chainsaw in all of your homestead builds. I even keep a small chainsaw handy when I'm doing masonry and carpentry jobs here in Alaska, although no *real* carpenter would ever dream of firing up a chainsaw while building a house. But guess what. You will, for many reasons. The question right now is, which saw am I going to recommend for you? First, let's be fair and show a list of chainsaw manufacturers we can choose from:

Black+Decker	DEWALT	Efco	Greenworks
Blue Max	Earthwise	EGO	Hitachi Koki
Craftsman	ECHO	Garwinner	Homelite

Husqvarna	McCulloch	Ryobi	Toro
ICS Blount	Milwaukee	Salem Master	WEN
Ivation	Oregon	Snapper	WORX
Jonsered	Poulan Pro	Stihl	Zombi
Kobalt	Redback	Sun Joe	
Makita	Remington	Tanaka	

OK. The first bit of experience I'm happy to share with you is this: Every single saw on this alphabetical list will, at some point, should you buy one, become used and get abused. It doesn't matter which you buy from this long list, it's gonna get broken. You'll drop it off the ladder. It will fall out of your truck. You'll fell a tree on it. You'll mix the gas wrong. You'll sharpen it wrong. You'll run over it. You'll break the pull cord. Your neighbor will borrow it. Or, God forbid, you'll work on it yourself . . . it's inevitable. The longer you own it, and the more trees you cut, the more likely one (or two) of the above scenarios will happen. And much sooner than you ever thought, that once-new saw will now need some maintenance, or a new chain, or maybe a new bar. Hold that thought.

So now let's cut . . . to the chase. Stihl, Husqvarna, and ECHO would be my top three recommendations for your new homestead saw. And here's why. Stihl seems to have more dealerships out there than anyone, and there are two Stihl dealerships within sixteen miles of my cabin. I also highly recommend Husqvarna, but honestly I don't even know of one qualified Husky dealer anywhere near me. Maybe in Anchorage? Well, I'm definitely not going to "town" if I don't have to . . . too far. And folks, that's my point. If there's a Husqvarna shop within sixteen miles of your house, then take a stroll down the aisle and pick out a saw. But as I've traveled (and worked . . .) with chainsaws extensively across North America, I have to say the Stihl dynasty is ubiquitous. Both Stihl and Husqvarna are extremely good saws, but whoever has the (hopefully reputable) dealership closest to your home is the one you need to consider.

And as for ECHO, it's a very reliable saw that often starts better than Stihl or Husky. ECHO saws are a bit less expensive than Stihl and Husky. I've seen a smattering of ECHO dealers out there, and I've had good experiences with the ECHO chainsaws (Jonsered is also a good saw). Whatever saw you choose needs to be sharpened to precision, and this is something you can do yourself with a round chainsaw file and a little practice. However, because saw chains are relatively inexpensive, you can buy several at a time, and when one becomes dull you can take it to the dealer (See? Not far away) to be sharpened. Currently, I have two saw chains at the Stihl dealership to be sharpened by them. I'm currently building a log home for someone and I hit two separate (steel) log screws with two separate chains (add that to our list of things that are inevitable). These were brand-new chains, and although I'm capable of sharpening them with a handheld saw file, the severe damage to the teeth warranted a saw sharpening machine to correct the trauma. As I write this, I'm sitting in my log cabin in Alaska that was built with both Stihl and Husqvarna saws (mainly Stihl).

I'm waiting for daylight to come so I can go to work on my other log cabin. Will the Stihl start in this cold? Yep. It's a crisp 6 degrees below zero outside, but the seasoned birch and spruce firewood is blazing away in the Blaze King woodstove. The cabin is warm and Little Su (our 140-pound Alaskan malamute) is basking on her favorite rug. This humble cabin has a second story, accessed by a log staircase. Mollee is making sourdough pancakes and about to set them on the kitchen bar, which is simply a live edge spruce tree slab countertop three inches thick. Wolf, salmon, and bear carvings accent the structural log posts and beams throughout this cabin. As you can "see," the chainsaw is integral in a homesteader's life. Without the chainsaw, we couldn't have risen from the ashes (and built this log home from the dead trees on the property) as fast as we did. And we wouldn't have this log staircase nor the ornate animal carvings. And right now, this cabin would be freezing cold and (they've just been served up) I'd be eating these (let me count . . . five) sourdough pancakes on a lackluster (and more expensive) Formica countertop. For nearly fifty years, I've scratched out a living in Alaska. And I've gone to work every day with an old wheelbarrow, a few basic masonry and carpentry hand tools, and . . . a chainsaw. That reminds me: Sun's up. Off to work.

> # The chainsaw is integral in a homesteader's life.

EXCAVATOR

What's your favorite color? I'll answer that for you: Your answer is . . . yellow. Well, it will be, the day a piece of "yellow iron" rolls onto your homestead. Nothing can transform a piece of land more than an excavator. A pad for a home, a well, a septic system, a pond, a large swath of heavily treed land, a driveway, or any seemingly insurmountable problem can be overcome with an excavator in just one day. I personally have built a road by scratching, scraping, and inching my way up a near-vertical cliff to twenty acres of inaccessible land on our homestead in Alaska. You can most likely figure out how to operate one on your own. But I recommend you have an experienced operator there to teach you, and more importantly, he or she will make use of your money and move some dirt while they educate you. Excavators rent by the day, week, or month. My suggestion is to evaluate your property, come up with a plan for the most urgent "heavy" tasks, then rent one for a week and put it to work. Imagine finding water, digging a pond, installing a septic system, clearing acres of forested land, burying all the stumps and brush or stacking them in a burn pile for winter, stockpiling black dirt separate from valuable gravel, and logging and stacking a mountain of large, heavy trees, in just one week. I do this on homestead after homestead all across North America. Just a few days with an excavator advances these homesteaders' lives, years into their homesteading dream.

Mastering an excavator takes time and practice; mastering a skid steer (also known as a Bobcat, after one of the most common models) takes less. A skid steer is a piece of construction equipment sized more like a car or pickup. It is most often equipped with a bucket and/or forks. You'll regularly see us operating them on *Homestead Rescue*, building roads and clearing land. When it comes to operating any piece of equipment, you will get to the point where you think you are a master. And guess what? You're not. At that exact moment, you're going to do some damage to your house, your vehicles, your property, the machine, and, God forbid, yourself.

Here's some advice from "someone" who has learned the hard way:

1. Be extremely careful working on any sloped or steep ground.

2. Never let the machine run out of fuel.

3. Clearing land with any type of equipment is the most dangerous thing you can do on a homestead—work methodically and be aware of your surroundings, especially people on the ground.

4. Be extremely cautious operating any equipment at full throttle. The faster the machine is running, the harder it is to avoid a mistake.

— NINE —

POWERING YOUR HOMESTEAD

O nce you have your living situation sorted, you've got a few other must-have items on your list. Number one is power, because frankly, you can't do much without it. Some homesteaders rely on generators, but ultimately this is a noisy, expensive, and frustrating way to keep the lights on. In the next few pages we'll go over your options for powering your house. But first, consider ways to add passive heating, cooling, and lighting. *Passive* means exactly that—energy that you can utilize and benefit from with no effort on your part (beyond the initial install). Passive is free, reliable, and has no moving parts, which means there is one less thing on the homestead that is going to require your time and attention.

PASSIVE SOLAR DESIGN

If you are building your own house, the number one consideration you want to make before you start your build is the orientation of the structure to the sun. This means making sure you have a significant southern exposure with most of your windows on this side. Two reasons: First, this will maximize the amount of sunlight—and heat—your house absorbs from the sun (low in the sky, and thus angled more directly at the windows) in the winter. Second, if you add an overhang to the roof, it will help *minimize* the amount of sunlight—and heat—your house absorbs in the summer (when the sun is higher in the sky, and thus blocked by the overhang). By putting your windows, and the most used areas of your house, along this southern exposure, you can keep your house either warm or cool simply by harnessing the power of the sun. In this scenario, you place bedrooms along the northern exposure of the house, since they are used less during the day and require less lighting.

For our house on the upper twenty acres, we designed it in a prow shape to maximize our sun exposure. The front of the house juts forward, with a large window on one side, our front door on the other, and a deep overhang above. Even on the coldest Alaska morning, the sun will begin the process of warming the house, raising the temperature a few degrees before we get to stoking the fire (we also have an oil-fired stove to keep the ambient temperature comfortably above freezing overnight). A friend in the window trade advised me to put in traditional tinted glass, to which I said, "No way!" Why would I want to weaken the warmth of the sun, or dim the beauty of our view? Turns out my friend had a valid point. The sun is so bright it is bleaching out the back of the couch against the window. Still, today, at 10 degrees above zero, I want all the passive heat I can get.

Here's another lesson we learned on the forty: Our first cabin, which burned down, was built at the base of a cliff on the lower part of the property. This location was incredibly cold. It didn't get enough sun, and the cliff essentially dammed the heavier cold air below it, meaning that counterintuitively it was *warmer* at a higher elevation. If you are building in a cold-weather environment, make sure you factor in how elevation and the topography of your land will affect the temperature of your property, and make sure you are picking the area with the best chance of staying (relatively) warm.

Most homesteaders (and often conventional architects) add elements called thermal masses to help store the heat that the house absorbs. Now, we've done this many times with greenhouses in cold climates, where we'll add black rocks to the walls of the structure. The theory is that they absorb heat during the day (either from the sun or from a wood-fired stove in a larger greenhouse), and radiate it slowly during the night. Within a house homesteaders try various tricks, like painting concrete floors or paving your floors and the lower part of your walls with a brick or stone accent wall.

Here's my issue with thermal masses: I'm working at home in late October, and the woodstove has been out for an hour or so. *Behind* my stove I have a wall of dark rocks, crystals, and fossils. According to the law of thermal mass, those materials should still be radiating heat, right? Not quite. When the fire goes out, the wall becomes stone cold. Many homesteaders use brick thermal mass around and on top of greenhouse stoves, sometimes stacking bricks, or using river rocks or other stones. Again, while these thermal masses have a benefit, it's not as big of a benefit as you might imagine from YouTube. In Alaska, you want to use every possible trick or hack to retain heat during a long winter, so we incorporate thermal masses in our builds, but I don't labor under the assumption they are going to dramatically change the temperature of my home.

Now, I'm one voice in a million, and plenty of homesteaders swear by their thermal mass. And frankly, even if they don't work as well as some might claim, a well-designed and -built stone or river-rock wall will add to the aesthetics of your home. I use stonework extensively to add to the look of our cabin (even adding dark slate heart-shaped inlays in the stone flooring). Bear in mind that a thermal mass will work against you during the summer (since it will still be holding and releasing heat). This technique works best in environments with a big difference in day and night temperatures (such as deserts in the western US) or in environments where the summer doesn't get overwhelmingly hot to begin with. Proceed with caution. And if your thermal mass is adding significant warmth and value to the homestead, congrats!

Some homesteaders also design their buildings to maximize natural light. You can see this at work in houses with a large bank of windows on the southern exposure of the second story or loft area. The light comes in and bounces off of the light-colored walls or ceiling to illuminate the interior. Moving into an existing structure? You can add solar tubes—basically cylindrical tubes with a half dome of plexiglass on the roof that refract and reflect light down into your house. However, I never recommend any type of skylight. If they're not installed correctly, I guarantee they will leak.

PASSIVE HEATING AND COOLING

Here's another essential: insulation. It's amazing how many freezing families we've met who are suffering because they haven't fully insulated their homes. In Pennsylvania we met a family living in a small cabin that had no insulation, *anywhere*. Their home had an empty loft space, and a large open crawl space under the cabin. The living area was cold enough that you had to wear a jacket, even when the stove was blazing. The dad was literally chopping wood from dawn to dusk, leaving precious little time for any other activities like caring for crops or livestock. We closed off the crawl space, added a drop ceiling, and fully insulated the loft. Now half an hour of chopping gave them enough wood for a few days, and Dad was free to get on with the real work of improving their land and caring for his family. Insulation is equally important in hot climates, to keep that cooler air in and the heat and humidity out.

Before you start thinking about how to actively heat or cool your home, it is essential that you do everything possible to passively heat and cool your home. The steps outlined above—orienting your build to a southern exposure, fully insulating your build, adding thermal mass, or even using the air system described earlier—can radically improve the quality of your life. Not only will they cut down on the time and money you spend actively heating or cooling, they will give you a backup in case of emergency. Remember, as a homesteader, you may be days away from a plumber's visit, or there might be a couple of feet of unplowed snow between you and the gas station should you need to refill your generator. A few degrees' difference in temperature can mean the difference between running water or frozen pipes.

SOLAR POWER

A standard solar power system.

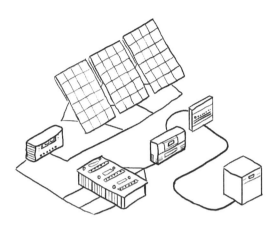

Living "off the grid" means just that: being disconnected and (perhaps) far removed from the labyrinth of transmission lines and power poles that cover our country. The impressive twenty-first-century advances in off-grid power systems, such as solar, wind, and hydro, have "enlightened" many people down the (well-lit) path to self-power. Thus, solar will be my first recommended off-grid power solution.

Check out this solar factoid: If you could harness the sun's energy (light) that blankets the surface of Planet Earth for just *one hour*, you would have captured enough energy to meet Planet Earth's power needs for *one year*. Impressive? Yep, and unlike my amazingly talented, likable, and . . . "bright" employees, I'm fairly confident that the sun is going to show up tomorrow morning, and right on time (even during hunting season, fishing season, bluegrass festivals, etc.).

Cloudy days are not a problem: You will still "get a charge" out of a clouded-over sun (albeit less power than a clear blue sky generates). In fact, I'm pretty sure that no matter where you live, the sun is rising, shining, and (after a long day) setting on your home's location. Should you have a row of solar panels pointed anywhere near that ball of fire (ninety-three million miles away) they will be absorbing light, creating photovoltaic electricity from the sun, and sending it through wires to an inverter mounted inside your cabin.

The sun bombards us—and our solar panels—with photons (light particles), the solar panels absorb that light, and the cell structure (silicone) of the panels excites electrons that begin to move, creating an electric current. The solar panels produce DC current, which is stored in your battery bank. An inverter converts the DC power into AC power; thus, your off-the-grid home can function exactly like any on-the-grid home. And the best part? There are no moving parts. This is a big deal: *Moving parts* mean *more problems*. Many homesteaders have set up bladed wind turbines only to be seriously disappointed by how quickly some wind products can fail. Why? A lot of moving parts, moving at high speed or with a lot of vibration, wear out (ask anyone over fifty).

For a person who's never lived off the grid before, it can be hard to believe that a simple solar array will provide enough energy to get through a day. So let's live "a day in the life of a homestead powered by the sun." As you enter through the front door, flip on the light. The house is wired exactly like every other house in North America, so the light bulb turns on like in any other house. The only difference is that the power to run this light bulb comes from the sun. Light bulbs don't actually require a lot of power, and the real test happens throughout the day when it's time to do a load of laundry, make dinner, or take a long hot shower—no problem. The electricity/appliance-dependent needs of a house on the grid can be met by that same house even if it is off the grid. Many water well pumps require 240 volts, as do all clothes dryers, but the sun is more than capable of meeting all the electricity needs of any house size or household.

The strides toward efficient, affordable off-grid solar power are yielding impressive results and significant industry growth. Oil and gas resources are finite, and in a hundred years or so have managed to pollute our planet. Why keep doing that? True, the upfront cost of solar power can start at ten thousand dollars and hit twice that (or more) fairly easily. Solar panels can come with a twenty-five-year warranty, or more. *But*, nearly all components needed to power your house from the sun are coming down in price every year, be it panels, invertors, or batteries. Solar power is the epitome of renewable energy. It's clean energy. It's silent. In the past, I wrestled with the financial commitment needed to go solar, but now I'm a true believer and proponent (and user) of all things solar. However, after moving to the highest point of our forty-acre homestead in Alaska to reap the full benefits of "The Land of the Midnight . . . Sun" (solar panels, garden, greenhouse, passive heat through deliberately south-facing windows of our log home), we are also well aware that this far north, one needs a backup generator to take the place of the ever-diminishing sunlight at summer's end. The generator will do exactly what the sun does, charge the batteries that ultimately run your house needs.

I'm approaching fifty years below zero (in Alaska) and have owned many a generator. Which one is best? Seems like I've tried them all, and, although Honda commands a higher price, after all these brutal winters working outside in the cold, Honda has indeed proven itself as the best-starting, most reliable, longest-running, and least noisy. In fact, it's surprisingly quiet. The Honda 5,000- and 7,000-watt generators come with wiring capabilities that make it easy to interface with your inverter, meaning, when the winter months provide less sunlight (photovoltaic—remember?), the battery levels will drop to 75 percent (seen on an LED panel), signaling the inverter to automatically start your generator. The generator will run nonstop until the battery charge levels reach 95 percent, at which point the inverter shuts off the generator until those charge levels drop back down to 75 percent again. It's not good for your batteries to consistently reach lower charge levels, especially lower than 50 percent.

And speaking of batteries, the most common types in America are lead acid, gel, AGM, and lithium. Lead acid batteries are inexpensive to make (using 160-year-old technology/ lead sulfuric acid), so they are the least expensive. But they do require regular maintenance, such as keeping up the water levels, and they do off-gas hydrogen and need to be vented outside. They also are usually larger in size, and those three things lead most people to the sealed battery choices of gel and AGM, as these batteries are maintenance-free, smaller in size, spill-proof, and nongassing. They withstand a wide range of temperatures and are considered nonhazardous, allowing them to be transported via rail, air, and road. I've had lead acid batteries that performed well, but I prefer gel/AGM batteries for said reasons. Also, they last longer than lead acid batteries. (Gel batteries are called that because they use silica sand as a base component that turns into a thick liquid. AGM stands for "absorbed glass mat." AGM is more efficient and outsells gel one hundred to one.)

Lastly, lithium batteries are amazing in every way, but are expensive. They can be 200 percent higher in price yet 60 percent lesser in weight. They have all the benefits of gel batteries, but are higher in energy, more stable, and able to be recharged hundreds of times. Recently, I looked hard at buying just ONE lithium battery that could more than store/ supply all of our homestead needs—at a cost of ten thousand dollars. Yep—for one, state of the art, latest, greatest lithium battery. I looked at my (six) perfectly functioning gel batteries, remembered they cost me a total of twelve hundred dollars, and decided to postpone that ten-thousand-dollar expenditure until my sealed AGM batteries wear out, which could easily be seven years.

Solar technology continues to get better as the efficiency of panels, inverters, and batteries increases, and solar systems are becoming more affordable. In the next seven years you will see an entire planet spinning toward more solar/battery dependency: cars, trucks, buildings, towns. You will see a continuation of the current urban exodus—millions of people leaving the cities in search of a better life. In fact, you may see *yourself* in those fleeing throngs seeking freedom, independence, and peace of mind. At the end of America's rural roads, so end the power poles, the overhead power lines, the grids. But for some, it's not the end of the road.

Robert Frost's "The Road Not Taken" beckons many, but no one regrets answering its call. For me, "two roads diverged": one on-grid, one off-grid. I looked down each, "sorry I could not travel both" as I "be one traveler." Both looked inviting, fulfilling. But the "road less traveled" had no poles or unsightly, sagging overhead wires. It seemed more intriguing, alluring, and challenging. Despite taking the harder road, it turns out that I can *still* have all the creature comforts of the on-grid road. How? Six solar panels, one 4,000-watt inverter, eight 6-volt batteries, and a very reliable energy source ninety-three million miles away. And now, thinking of the other road choice, "I doubted if I should ever come back." So, in poetic conclusion:

Two roads diverged in a wood, and I—

I took the one less traveled by,

And that [solar power] has made all the difference.

WIND POWER

Remember seeing all those classic windmills spinning away next to the farmhouses across America? I believe one million of those windmills were once (and many still are) pumping up water from deep down in the ground, without the use of electricity. Wind power is nothing new to farmers, homesteaders, and ranchers. Indeed, the *invisible* wind gave life by pumping the *essential* water from the ground.

These nostalgic prairie icons of the nineteenth and twentieth centuries set the precedent for the huge windmill farms cropping up now in the twenty-first century, as they all use the same technology. A blade is designed to capture the optimum amount of wind to turn it, much like a sail on a boat (or the wing of a bird or aircraft). The moving wind turns the blades of a propeller that is attached to a shaft, which ultimately spins a generator fast enough to create electricity. Ever stick your hand out of the car window doing 60 mph? Exactly. That's powerful, clean, kinetic energy. However, most people don't have a steady

60 mph wind blowing at their property, not that you would want that anyway. Wind turbines are designed to generate power at wind speeds as low as 6 to 9 mph, and most wind turbines are designed to shut down at 55 mph to prevent damage to the unit.

So, when considering wind power, the main question is: Does *your* house location qualify or justify the purchase of a wind generator? Is there enough wind? Go to windexchange .energy.gov for starters. This resource will give you relevant statistics about the amount of wind you can expect—and the speed you can expect it to blow at—for any place in America. You can also calculate your power needs in relation to your annual wind speeds. For example, the best states for wind power are Texas, Iowa, Kansas, Oklahoma, and California. The worst states for wind power are Alabama, Arkansas, Florida, Louisiana, Georgia, Kentucky, Mississippi, Virginia, and North Carolina. Other states with light wind are Delaware, New Jersey, and Connecticut. Do the research before you get too excited, and keep in mind that ALL of the aforementioned states (and the rest of the planet) got plenty of sun, and solar power is a secure option.

For those people in areas where winds are blowin' aplenty, you'll need to pick that optimum spot to set your tower. Do not attach it to your roof, as there is significant vibration and noise from a wind turbine. The vibration will transfer itself throughout the hard framing of your house, and trust me when I say you can actually feel it inside your home. And don't think for a second that all residential wind turbines are quiet. Make sure you settle on that company that specializes in "less noisy." I have been on many an off-grid location (from Alaska to Texas) and found the remote, beautiful, naturally symphonic silence broken by the out of tune accompaniment of a whining wind turbine, or worse, the constant single bass note (drone) of a gas or diesel generator running 24/7. There are impressively quiet wind turbines on the market, so find one . . . especially if you have any neighbors with good hearing.

How tall should the tower be before you mount the wind turbine atop it? At least thirty feet tall, and it should be the tallest object within a three-hundred-foot radius. Some companies recommend the tower's height be sixty-five feet, others recommend ninety feet (and a six-hundred-foot radius). In fact, the experts say the sweet spot is from eighty feet to 120 feet. The point: The higher you go, the more (smooth) wind you will encounter. And the higher you go, the less noise you will hear.

You can already see the challenges involved should you commit to a tower/wind turbine installation. Consider the costs as well. Often the tower install alone can be

50 percent (or more) of completion costs. Yes, the wind is "free," but is there enough of it (in your area) to justify the investment? Many people have complained about their wind generator system, blaming the company they bought it from because of poor performance. But, many of these people have placed these wind generators at an unrecommended ten- or twenty-foot height. They may get excited seeing it spinning for the first time, but at that low height the only wind hitting the blades is "dirty wind," or wind that has become turbulent after it has passed over or through trees or buildings that disrupt the smooth, steady (more powerful) wind flow. Read the manual: It's not kidding when it tells you that the minimum tower height is thirty feet and that the recommended height is sixty feet or higher. One exception: If you live on the plains, in the desert, or in a treeless area with zero obstructions (for smooth wind to become dirty) you certainly could put that turbine at twenty feet because it would be getting hit with smooth, clean air, and that unobstructed air carries the optimum wind power.

Think about a regular house fan. You plug it in, the electric motor spins the blades, and you make sure nothing is in the way so you can feel the full effect of the smooth, cool, blowing air. Now think of that fan sequence in reverse. To reap the full power of the wind, nothing should be in the way of smooth, unobstructed air coming *into* the (fan) blades. Once they start rotating, they turn a generator that produces electricity. However, even in perfect, smooth wind conditions, the wind alone can't spin the blades fast enough to generate usable power for your house. During favorable wind conditions, the propeller blades spin at around 400 rpm. But a generator needs 1,200 to 1,800 rpm to produce electricity. Not to worry. A gearbox is placed between the blades and the generator, increasing the rpms from 400 to 1,800.

The number of rotations per minute allows the wind-driven blades to generate power. And remember that old bicycle-riding saying, "Look Mom, no hands!!" You'll be saying it in a different context if you get too close to these blades. Another reason for not mounting a wind generator under thirty feet of elevation. It's interesting to note that the wind must travel completely *through* the blades to generate power. How efficient is a wind turbine? You'll be surprised to learn that only 30 to 50 percent of the wind hitting a propeller is captured as power. In fact, the "theoretical maximum" wind one can harness is 59 percent. But that said, in a perfect world wind power is a clean, renewable resource. It's also cost effective and occupies a very small space on your land. And if you buy a quality system, you can experience low maintenance. Once you have the tower/wind generator installed, the wire going into your house is carrying the exact same DC current as a set of solar panels. Meaning, a set of batteries is needed to store that power and an inverter to change that (wind-powered) DC current into the AC format that a normal house needs to operate household appliances. Wind generators require the exact setup that a set of solar panels needs.

So whether you've chosen solar or wind (or both) to power your home, know this: If it's solar, it starts with the sun and ends with . . . you. If it's wind power, it starts with the wind and ends with . . . you. *You* are the deciding factor. What to choose, how to design, where to install, and how to maintain. I'll guarantee you this: The sun and wind won't let you down. Reciprocate.

WATER POWER

Alaska has three million lakes, twelve thousand rivers, and 46,600 miles of shoreline. There's plenty of water but very few (residential) people actually use that water to make electricity. Why? Let's start with . . . me. I live on a wild and turbulent river, yet I haven't figured out a viable hydropower system . . . yet. This river fluctuates in elevation, floods, has a pristine (and protected) king salmon run, sees temperatures drop to 30 degrees below zero, and gets three feet of ice and four feet of snow. Now, visualize *anything* on the market that will generate hydropower to meet all of our modest electricity needs. I've looked. It doesn't exist. True, I have built water wheels that generated power in other states. Ironically, I've also built one about five miles downriver from us (with some help from Dave, the Smartest Homesteader I Know) on our river. But I've never been fully satisfied with the end result: a romantic, aesthetic, creative water wheel that in reality can't produce enough power to run a legitimate cabin's electrical needs.

First, anyone in cold climates needs to know the water, and the wheel, are most likely going to freeze during the winter months. In Alaska, that's potentially seven months. Second, salmon, kayakers, rafters, and the government are way ahead of you, meaning it may not be legal to install a water wheel or other types of hydro in your river or stream. But wait . . . so now you're going to extract that water to run some type of generator on shore? Well, that removal or displacement of water can also be "illegal." Remember when we talked about water rights? If you are in a state with water scarcity issues, people are going to look sideways at any impediment or pollutant to that all-important resource, even if it's as simple as briefly moving small amounts of water to power your wheel.

However, if there are no spring, creek, or river water restrictions, you can start looking at how to extract some power from your moving water. Hydropower is water power, and the more water pressure you build, the more water power you can generate. The pressurized water hits the impeller of a turbine, causing it to spin, and because that (now spinning) turbine is connected to a generator, it spins fast enough to generate power. The two most common residential micro-hydro systems are impulse types (jet force), such as Pelton and Turgo wheels. Kaplan is a reaction design, and Francis is a hybrid of both. All will generate power, but relative design differences are available because all water flow, speed, fall, and volume vary (as do properties and power needs).

For example, if you have high head (the amount of height the water "falls") pressure and low flow rate, use a Pelton wheel. But if you have low head pressure and high flow, use a Kaplan. Francis is designed for medium head, medium flow. Technically, all your technology bases are covered. Again, no matter what hydro system you need and choose, you will still have to bring that power into the house and store it in a battery bank, and change that DC power into AC power through an inverter.

Solar, wind, and hydropower all need power storage (batteries) and power conversion (inverters). It's fairly easy to produce 12-volt electricity with any hydro system, including alternators taken from a car or truck motor. Even 24-volt systems may be within your modest hydro system investment. But if you're trying to get 48-volt, 60 amps or more, and enough to run a 240-volt dryer and 240-volt well pump at the same time, you're going to have to have enough water, a good design, and a significant hydro unit. So hydropower is very doable, but hydropower twelve months a year is not doable for the huge off-grid demographic that experiences freezing temperatures in winter. That includes me, and most likely you. It can be done, but you have to be pretty determined and ready to spend some money if you're going to truly outsmart Mother Nature.

The one water wheel we've constructed on the show—near my own home in Alaska— was a viable solution for the small cabin. We were able to get around the rules and regulations by constructing the water wheel on a pontoon, meaning it was not fixed and could be removed from the water during the winter, or at the command of the local authorities should they demand it. Finally, the homeowner had the skills and ability to maintain it.

SOLAR WATER HEATERS

Active solar water heaters use pumps to circulate the heat. These heaters are fitted onto your southern facing roof and use a series of tubes to run water through them, absorbing the sun's heat and in turn heating the water. They are (understandably) more expensive and not something the average homesteader without specialized skills will be able to make on their own. Passive solar water heating systems, on the other hand, are relatively simple to DIY. These heaters—also known as batch heaters—use tanks painted black and stored within insulated boxes that face south. There are multiple different configurations of batch water heaters, depending on the amount of water you need and your DIY abilities. However, they all follow the same principle. The southern exposure of the box is glazed (you can use discarded windows or buy new material), allowing for the maximum amount of light to be absorbed by the black barrels and warm the water within them. As the water heats up, it moves up a series of barrels. When the water enters the house it is already warm, and a conventional water heater takes this warm water and brings it up to a suitable temperature for showering. Passive heating or cooling is less about bringing temperatures "all the way" to a comfortable number. Instead, they get you part or most of the way there, meaning your active heating and cooling systems don't have to work as hard, and you don't have to stress as hard about the money and resources going into heating or cooling your house and water.

ACTIVELY HEATING YOUR HOME

Power is one thing, but you also need a reliable and consistent heat source. On the upper twenty acres we have a modern woodstove with a catalytic converter that regulates the heat moving up through the chimney, preventing it from getting too hot. We have an oil-fired stove on the other side of the cabin as backup, which prevents the cabin from freezing when we aren't there to keep the wood-fired stove going. This setup allows me to safely leave the house in my dual jobs as contractor and on *Homestead Rescue*, safe in the knowledge that Mollee, and our house, will stay warm and the pipes won't freeze.

This also speaks to another issue: We are living in the modern world, and there is no reason to pass over improvements in safety, convenience, or comfort simply because that's how old-timers did it. Older is not necessarily better. Catalytic converters are relatively new, and they can drastically lower the temperature that a stove has to reach in order for the materials within it to combust. When that heat rises up through your chimney, it's 500 degrees as opposed to 1,100. Not only are they safer, they use less fuel, because they burn it more efficiently. And when you are heating your stove with wood, you don't want to cut one extra piece of firewood if you don't have to.

Once you've had a house burn down because your forty-year-old woodstove allowed the chimney pipe to reach heat levels beyond its design (igniting something in the roof system), you will never own a used woodstove again for the rest of your life, and

Older is not necessarily better.

likewise, you will never recommend an older, used woodstove or chimney pipe to anyone, ever. When Maciah and Misty built their amazing log home on the lower twenty, I noticed that they purchased a used woodstove to heat their cabin. However, after our house burned down and without any prompting from me, Maciah and Misty replaced their used woodstove, buying a state-of-the-art Blaze King woodstove off the showroom floor of our local dealer. Smart move, guys. The lesson here is to be wary of used woodstoves and used chimney pipes. Although I recommend repurposing and upcycling whenever possible, chimneys and stovepipes are one area to avoid cutting corners.

ROCKET STOVE

Recently we worked with a family who had a straw house that they were heating with a rocket stove. The rocket stove is similar in concept to the rocket stove bathtub. They burn small pieces of wood and are generally considered to be fuel-efficient ways to heat houses or operate small portable stoves. When they're used to heat a house, homesteaders build up large thermal banks of brick, cinder block, or adobe (though again: I personally don't believe those thermal masses do as much as people claim). I would obviously recommend a woodstove before I would recommend a rocket stove, especially in colder climates where heating your home is critical.

When homesteaders ask me about these stoves, my response is to ask, Why use outdated technology when vastly better alternatives are available to you? Yes, a rocket stove will keep your house warm, but they are less safe, are less efficient, take up more space, and are less environmentally sound than a modern stove. During our first moments in the house, one of our team managed to dislodge a large chunk of the stove with his boot. Bear in mind, this was a *straw house*. Having just had a house go up in flames, I'm inclined to think that any stove you can damage just by walking into it is not a wise choice.

WHICH TYPE OF HEATING SYSTEM TO CHOOSE?

Given the choice between any type of solar heater or woodstove, I will choose the woodstove. Given a choice between any type of rocket stove and a gravity-fed (no electricity), oil-fired heating stove, I will choose the oil-fired drip stove. Given the choice between any type of solar hot water heater and a propane-fired hot water heater on-demand unit, I will choose the propane-fired hot water heater on-demand unit. Period. There are many woodstoves to choose from, and as said, we've chosen Blaze King. When it comes to gravity-fed, oil-fired heating stoves, we've chosen Kuma stoves. We also have to mention Toyo stoves here, as they are found in thousands of homes here in Alaska. And when it comes to heating water, I recommend Rinnai propane-fired hot water on-demand units. In our nearly fifty years in Alaska, we've had our share of roughing it.

What I'm recommending to you here are the very devices that operate daily on our forty-acre off-grid homestead in Alaska. If I thought there was a better system, I'd have it, and I would be recommending it to you. The bottom line: I'm trying to make your homestead life the best it can be. Heat. Hot water. Don't drink the YouTube Kool-Aid. Be warm and safe, and have hot water on demand 24/7, 365 days a year.

Wood-fired stove: When you're heating with wood, you'll see the importance of having an efficient, properly sized, safe woodstove.

TEN

GARDENS AND COMPOST

The key to a bountiful homestead isn't large acreage. The key lies squarely in a good plan, some basic knowledge, and a willingness to learn as you go. This underscores the potential of smaller homesites, and should be encouraging to those on a shoe-string budget. But here's the deal. No homestead is completely self-sufficient. Most home-steaders I know go to the grocery store on a regular basis. Look at us. We have cans and cans of preserved pickles, tomatoes, salmon, and various game meat. *And bananas, and apples, and ice cream in the fridge.* I drink coffee, and we certainly aren't growing that on the forty.

Growing your own food is less about growing everything you need than it is about figur-ing out what will grow well, and harvesting as much of that as you can through the growing season. Although spread out from each other, all of our developments thus far could easily fit on one acre, including the log cabin, garden, greenhouse, chicken coop, and goat pen. And we're producing a lot of food, goat's milk, and a dozen eggs a day. How much property do you need? Some have studied and calculated that as much as sixty thousand pounds of organic foods could be grown on just one acre of land per year. No matter how small or big the farm-ing footprint, every homestead and homesteader will be different, lending an unfettered creative license to each and all. Yours is truly an original, a manifested dream come true. After just one year of growing food, your knowledge will increase by light-years. You'll see what you did right; you'll know what you did wrong.

Add this to your pivotal moments of off-grid living: As significant and memorable as it is seeing your first light switch activate a bulb powered by the sun, or seeing clean drinking water (or hot water, for that matter) come out of a fixture inside your home, trust that see-ing your first green sprout(s) emerge from richly black dirt will be momentous. Success in gardening is well within reach of anyone, if you follow a few simple steps. First, choose the best location. South-facing allows for more sun, crucial to the growing process. Is a water source nearby? Is an outbuilding close enough for rain catchment? Having enough water can make or break your success.

Do not minimize the importance of a tall fence. Everything from rabbits to moose will want to participate in your garden's harvest time. The type and height of your "defense" are relative to the size, agility, and IQ of the respective intruder. Longtime Alaskan Dave Newcomb has enormous six-foot-tall fences surrounding huge, impressive gardens. But last year while he was working alone inside his food fortress, a moose jumped the six-foot wall and grazed undaunted (and unwanted) at will. Moose, on the average, weigh in at more than a thousand pounds and stand six feet at their shoulder. Right now, a large female moose is living on the edges of Dave's homestead and has even charged him a few times. You most likely won't have a moose problem, but I guarantee that something in your area will need to be fenced out.

Once the garden footprint and fence are in place, it's time to focus on your soil. You'll need to determine the pH level of your soil water. pH levels range from 0 to 14. A pH level of 7 is neutral; a pH level of less than 7 is acidic, whereas a pH level of greater than 7 is alkaline. Old-timers tested their soil by placing a small sample in a bowl of vinegar. If it fizzes, you have alkaline soil. Conversely, add some baking powder to a damp soil sample. If it fizzes, you have acidic soil. These days soil tests are cheap and easy to find, so back up your results with a test from Lowe's, just to be sure.

I distinctly remember a determined homesteader in Kentucky who spent five years trying to develop a garden. Despite his efforts, and changing the location of the garden several times, he was only able to grow one bell pepper in five years. After hearing this puzzling tale we immediately tested the soil, something he had never done (in five years). The results were telling. The entire area had been stripped years earlier by coal miners. When the mining companies were done, they reclaimed huge tracts of land (restored the terrain, planted grass), and at first glance, it all looked inviting. But just beneath those fields of beautiful grass were contaminants that kept this deserving family from growing food. Oh—except for that one pepper. Adding lime, minerals, or fertilizer to those tainted fields seemed like a bad idea. We opted for some much higher ground that would involve substantial tree removal and days of hard work. But before committing to ANY work, we took soil samples and had them tested. We found no contamination, and pH levels of 6. Perfect. We terraced the pristine, virgin high ground, fenced it in, and planted every vegetable you can think of, including bell peppers. A simple pH test would have saved them from five years of frustration.

The cure for a low pH number is lime. Twenty to fifty pounds of lime per one thousand square feet will bring your pH back to optimum food-growing soil (ten to twenty-five pounds per five hundred square feet, etc.). Be careful—too much lime can lead to nutrient deficiencies and swing your pH levels too high. The best way to introduce lime to your garden area is to first spread it evenly and then rake it into the top two inches of soil. A walk-behind drop spreader works best, and a tiller may speed up the process once applied to the soil surface. Winter months are the best time for this. Most vegetables will thrive once this step is followed, but it should be noted that not all plants need lime. Never lime potatoes or tomatoes. Many flowers *need* the more acidic soil and fare poorly with lime. A pH level of 5.5 to 7 seems to be a generic, safe window for most garden vegetables.

You don't need a degree in chemistry (although it would help) when planting a garden, but you do need a basic understanding of your soils. It's relatively easy to amend your soil for growing success. If you don't prepare the soil first, you will see the error of your ways at harvest time, manifested as you dig up two-inch-long carrots and see unhealthy, nutrient-deficient broccoli, cauliflower, and peas. There's a variety of do-it-yourself pH test kits, but many opt to have a lab do the testing at a cost ranging from twenty to four hundred dollars. Every year garden soils need to be retested, refertilized, retilled, and reweeded.

AILING SOIL, AND HOW TO FIX IT

If, like our friends with the bell pepper, your soil is hopelessly contaminated, you have two choices: Walk away from that part of your property, or attempt the long and slow process of rebuilding your soil. This philosophy is at the heart of regenerative agriculture. Anyone who relies on growing their own plants to eat understands how crucial it is to have good topsoil, but America loses an astonishing 1.69 billion tons of topsoil *per year.* Since settlers arrived, we have lost an average of almost seven inches of topsoil coverage, sometimes in big, catastrophic events like the Dust Bowl, but more frequently in smaller, more localized disasters such as the midwestern floods of 2019. Boiled down, the key to good, healthy soil is organic matter and the microbial organisms that feast off it. Not only is it better for growing, this "live" soil is vastly more flood resilient. In fact, a 1 percent increase in organic matter makes soil capable of holding thousands of gallons more water per acre. If the soil can hold on to the water, there is less runoff, less leaching of nutrients, and less flooding.

Other regenerative agriculture practices to consider are limiting tilling (which breaks up the soil, leading to more erosion) and using cover crops and rotational grazing to add carbon back into the soil. If your soil is contaminated, you can plant cover crops such as sunflower, corn, or alfalfa, or put in fast-growing trees like willows and poplars to pull some of the contaminants out of the ground. This method is known as *phytoremediation* and has been practiced by farmers since the 1940s. What you plant depends on what your problem is, so do a detailed soil test to find out exactly what you are dealing with. Once you know, you can do the research to find the right plant for what ails you. Alpine pennygrass, for instance, can remove the highly toxic cadmium at ten times the rate of any other plant. Indian grass pulls up huge amounts of pesticide residue. Willow roots can accumulate large amounts of heavy metals from areas that have been doused with diesel fuel. Bear in mind that these plants don't stop removing matter from the soil when you want them to—research found that broccoli removed *too many* useful metals from the soil. It's all about balance, and paying attention, and repeated testing until your soil is in the shape you want it to be.

The contamination was so extensive for the family mentioned above that this method would have taken years, and it may never have gotten the soil back to a healthy place (still, it's a good start). But if your land has a relatively small area of contamination (perhaps from an old structure that leaked unknown substances into the soil), this method can help alleviate the situation. Remember: You won't want your animals eating the cover crops, and you won't want to plow them under either. Current research suggests that sunflowers that have been used to pull lead from the soil need to be incinerated, although some studies claim that the seeds are still safe for consumption, since the majority of the metals are stored in the stems and leaves of the plant. As always—read, and ask questions that apply to your specific circumstances, before you start.

THE GARDENING RESURGENCE

Once you know your soil is primed and ready to go, it's time to think about your garden. Statistics prove there has been a resurgence in gardening, most likely driven by an awareness of organic food health benefits. And more and more people are taking a vested interest in where their food is coming from. *The National Gardener* claims that gardeners in general grew by 17 percent and the millennial demographic alone grew by 63 percent. COVID-19 has played a significant role in this, as people are spending much more time at home and are using that time to develop gardens and erect greenhouses. "The times they are a-changin'," which has incited an urban exodus of masses seeking a simple life wherein self-grown, organic, whole foods are fundamental.

Plants are a lot like people: each one with its own needs, personality, and quirks. Some need more attention. Some prefer more sun. Some prefer shade. Some need their own space. And their health and well-being become your responsibility. Trial and error will come and go, and by your second year at gardening you will see a marked improvement. Greener, bigger, healthier plants will fulfill the "vegetables" of your labor.

The most popular garden vegetables are broccoli, carrots, cauliflower, cabbage, cucumbers, beans, lettuce, peas, zucchini, squash, and tomatoes. Each has its own best time to plant and best time to harvest. Each has its own "how to plant" and "how to harvest." Each has its "favorite" spot in the garden layout. And remember this when planting seeds: Look at the size of a seed and plant it in the soil at twice that thickness. For example, a seed 1/16" in size would need to be planted 1/8" deep. Every seed packet will bear instructions on how to plant it and at what depth. Some wing it with a "plant everything a quarter inch deep" rule, but that may be a bit deep for best sprouting results.

Forget to water the flowers? They will let you know with their drooping leaves, disheveled petals, and weak stems. Subsequently, the question for Gardening 101 is, when to water and how much? As for when, morning is best because the plants will have time to absorb the life-sustaining water before the rising sun also raises the day's temperature. The heat of the day will rob the ground of moisture, impacting the plants' potential growth rate. People who choose to water a garden in the evening may increase the chances of a fungus or a disease developing. As for how much water to use on those mornings? As always, it depends on the plants. But whether a seedling or that hundred-pound cabbage (Alaska holds the current world record for a cabbage, weighing in at 138.25 pounds), it's the same rule. Make sure the water is absorbed by the soil, not just pooled up on the surface. Roots go down in search of life-giving water. Get to know your plants intimately, much like a circle of friends. Greener, bigger, healthier, happier plants will greet you at the garden gate (sufficiently tall). "Dew" it. I'm rooting for you.

WORM FARMS AND COMPOST HEAPS

Your success as a gardener is all about the soil. If you want to grow a lot of plants and harvest a lot of vegetables, you need to fortify your soil. The obvious answer is compost, and most homesteads have either a compost bin or a compost pile. The bin system has the benefit of repelling rodents, pests, or (maybe) predators who are intrigued by the smells coming from your decomposing food scraps. The pile is easy to manage—just throw on what you have and mix it in. However, you may find that rats, raccoons, or other animals can quickly become a problem. We use two kinds of compost (and don't actually have a compost pile or bin, which will be explained below): worm and leaf.

Just inside of our back door is a small black plastic box. This is Mollee's worm farm, populated by thousands of red wigglers (*Eisenia foetida*). She diligently feeds and cares for them with vegetable scraps and other food items. Our farm is particularly healthy and active: She feeds it roughly half a pound of food a day. In the summer the worm farm lives outdoors, but as soon as the temperatures start to dip, they come in for winter as they won't survive freezing (their temperature range is between 50 and 80 degrees Fahrenheit). Worm farms generate vermicast, also known as worm humus or worm manure. This substance is generally rich in nitrogen, phosphate, and potassium—the key elements of any fertilizer. How much of each of these substances you get depends on the worms' diet. Worms are key to regenerative agriculture. A "happy" worm farm is one where the worms are reproducing, doubling their population every ninety days or so, producing compost, and, most important, not producing any foul odors. Just as with a composting toilet, you know you have a problem if you can smell it.

When you have healthy worm populations in your garden, they serve multiple purposes. One, outlined above, is breaking down organic matter into those three key compounds. Worms can process as much as *fifteen tons per acre* of organic matter every year. As they do this, they burrow through the soil, making the soil more porous and allowing the water to percolate down through the soil rather than pooling on the surface. (Critical, if you remember back to our flash flooding chapter.) These passages also oxygenate the soil, so even deep roots are getting the oxygen they need to survive. As the worms travel through the soil, they drag subsoil up to the surface, mixing it with the more organic-rich topsoil and ensuring the nutrients spread throughout the different layers of soil. Finally: Worm "slime" is both nitrogen rich (good fertilizer) *and* helps form small clumps of soil known as aggregates, which encourage airflow throughout the soil.

As those worms reproduce, you can introduce them into your garden, making what's called a vermiculture bed. The purpose of this is to give your worms the chance to get to work in your garden, doing everything outlined above: improving the soil structure, enriching it with natural fertilizer, fortifying it against flooding, and enhancing the overall health of the garden. A vermiculture bed is essentially a large worm farm, dug into the soil and structured around layers of newspaper, compost scraps, hay, mulch, and topsoil. Alternatively, you can make an in-bed composter, essentially a two- or five-gallon bucket worm farm with the bottom removed, so it's an open cylinder that is dug into the garden bed and buried up to the lid. The worms move between the kitchen scraps in the bucket and the garden bed, spreading the compost out from the bucket throughout the growing area. The lid protects the food scraps from pests and insects.

Worms are essential to a healthy and productive garden, so however you do it, make sure you take the time to encourage and care for your worm population. Be mindful of temperature and moistness. Temperature and humidity extremes will kill your worms, so bring them inside when it is too hot or too cold, and don't let them drown or dry out (if you have a bed or in-ground worm farm, the worms will burrow deep to avoid temperature extremes).

LEAVES OF GRASS

After worms, the next best compost on Planet Earth is leaves. And the best thing to do with leaves? *Leave* . . . them in place. Fruit trees, ash, poplar, maple, and willow all make valuable compost, as their leaves are rich in calcium and nitrogen. Decomposing leaves are vital to your soil, and to the insect life that makes its home there. The roots find the best nutrients in the soil, and their goal is to send it all the way up that tree to the leaves. Those leaves in turn are packed with the nutrients that the next generation of plants and trees need to survive. The forest is alive because of leaves, and when they fall they do double duty, breaking down into mulch and insulating the ground around the tree. If you're a homesteader you're probably not too worried about maintaining a well-manicured lawn. Good, since a suburban lawn, cleared of all leaf and grass clippings, is about as unnatural and unhealthy an environment as possible.

So leave a good layer of leaves around your trees and on the ground. Where you have enough to spare, gather them up to make the backbone of your compost heap. Successful compost and gardening strategy is taking advantage of all your potential resources: Don't waste anything. Add in grass clippings that haven't been fertilized. Manure is next: Goat, then horse manure is the best. Goat manure is the gold standard, and you can use it almost immediately. The smell is (once again) a good giveaway: Your goat manure should smell earthy and not offensive. When it reaches that stage, it's ready. Duck manure is terribly pungent and not fun to smell. Chicken manure is literally too hot; if you put it on your garden, it will kill the plants. Let it break down for at least a year before you use it as fertilizer.

COMPOST PESTS

Finally, you can add in all those household food waste items: eggshells, coffee grounds, vegetable scraps, and so on. This leads us to an important point: If you have food in your compost that was once good enough for you to eat, animals are going to think, *Well, it's still good enough for me.* Some composters add fishbones to their compost pile, and an even smaller group believe it's OK to add meat and bones occasionally. For very obvious reasons this is not a good idea: Anything like meat, fish, or bones will draw in predators. We don't have a compost pile—even though I heartily recommend them for most homesteads—for the simple reason that we have too many bears, lynx, bobcats, and wolves in our vicinity. Anything that smells interesting to a predator is doubly dangerous in an area like ours, where our neighbors are hungry and plentiful. At one point we had ducks, and their pungent

Bear: With over 600,000 bears in North America, it is highly likely one of them lives in your neighborhood, and they were there first. Respect.

manure pulled in predators. Bears can smell 2,100 times better than a human. This summer we had two brown bears and one black bear visit our home that we know of. A foul-smelling compost pile would most likely invite more of each.

HUGELKULTUR

Our garden has a greenhouse, illustrated here, and a fenced-in garden. Running through the garden is a large mound, about waist high, that in the summer is covered in zucchini,

Greenhouse: Regardless of the design, make sure it is south-facing to maximize sunlight. Since many greenhouses actually get too hot, incorporate sufficient ventilation.

cucumbers, squash, pumpkins, and other vining plants. This is a German concept called a *hugelkultur* (often called a "hugul culture" in the American homesteading community), which originated out of the regenerative agriculture movement of the last century and is a great homestead technique to make the most of the short growing season in a northern climate.

At its simplest, a hugelkultur bed takes advantage of heat and nutrients generated in an organic compost heap. The log, branch, and leaf layers host insects, fungi, and microorganisms, and their rotting and decaying process provides all kinds of nutrients. A hugelkultur can last decades, though as it ages it will slowly shrink down and eventually will need to be rebuilt. Hugelkulturs also have the benefit of retaining water, which cuts down on watering. Our hugelkultur is so productive that we sometimes end up with more squash, zucchini, and gourds than we can either eat, can, or preserve. Not a bad problem to have. At the end of the growing season, Mollee covers it with a layer of straw and it "sits out" the winter, waiting for late spring, when she plants the warm and nutrient-rich hugelkultur with new starts, and the process begins all over again.

GREENHOUSES

We've built greenhouses everywhere from the Deep South to the Arctic North. For those of you in the northern climes, a well-functioning greenhouse is essential, and, if you choose to heat it, it can be in use for a substantial part of the year. Even if you are in a temperate climate, a greenhouse can expand your growing season and give you flexibility to have fresh greens year-round. In Arizona, we added a greenhouse onto an elderly couple's living structure, in part to make access-

Greenhouse framing: Whether it's built out of wood or steel or plastic pipes, be aware of potential snow loads come the winter season.

ing and tending to the plants easier on them as they grew older. The family with the house made out of thirty thousand tires had an indoor ditch running under floor-to-ceiling windows that lined their long southern exposure. You guessed it: That indoor ditch is now their indoor greenhouse. So get creative, and devise a greenhouse that works for your needs and the realities of your property.

As you plan your greenhouse, first figure out the major challenges you and your plants will be facing: Is it excessive cold, lack of water, intense heat? Any of these issues will require some creative thinking to solve, so the first thing to consider is that your greenhouse doesn't necessarily need to look like a greenhouse. If you are living in an area with a harsh and unforgiving winter, you can try the thermal mass concept to keep your plants warm enough to survive during the dark, cold months. For one family in Montana, that meant building the greenhouse into a small cave on the side of a rock cliff face: The cliff had great southern exposure, and the rocks were naturally black. Once we glassed off the front of the cave, the couple had a greenhouse that retained enough heat overnight to keep the plants alive until sunbreak. Whether it was the thermal mass or the fact that the walls naturally insulated the plants from the colder temperature outside the cave is open for debate.

No cave? Then you'll want to dig down, partially burying your greenhouse in a four-foot hole. The purpose of this is twofold: First, by digging down you'll reach a layer of earth that is naturally warmer than a greenhouse sitting on the surface (it's the same principle that can heat and cool your living structure as discussed in a previous chapter). In these instances, we added large rocks into the walls to hold up the structure, since they were there, and we painted them black in the hopes they might retain some heat.

In extreme climates like ours, greenhouses will need to be heated if you want to grow year-round (another option is to attach your greenhouse to the side of your dwelling, sharing heat between the two areas). Solar heating is an option for smaller greenhouses; larger greenhouses may require their own heating system, like a wood-burning stove.

A more conventional greenhouse is a relatively simple build. If you have access to a local junkyard or rebuilding center (where salvaged house materials are sold), you can source the windows for your build cheaply (frankly, I'm amazed how often you can find a homeowner or builder who is happy to donate windows they are swapping out and have no use for—keep your ears open and spread the word in the local community that you are looking for them). Keep an eye open for hinged casement windows that will allow you to open and close the greenhouse, venting hot air and encouraging circulation depending on the conditions.

EXCESS CROPS

Many homesteaders have a dream of never going to the grocery store again. I'm here to tell you: You will. Nearly every homesteading family I've met is still making semi-regular trips to stock up on food and supplies. Rather than trying to grow everything, focus on growing the crops you have the most success with, and supplement those with items you can buy at the store.

One other strategy is to focus on either selling what you can easily grow or bartering your surplus for those additional supplies. I'm here to tell you this is harder, and vastly more time and energy laborious, than you might think. Frankly, many homesteaders find growing extra crops to sell to be too much work for too little reward. However, *if* you are close enough to a local market, have a crop that can be dried and shipped, or have a bartering network to tap into, cash for crops can add to your bottom line.

Over the years we've set families up to grow everything from rice to fruit. As always, you want to take advantage of the specific qualities of your land, even if they don't seem like qualities at first. Our rice-growing family was plagued by floods and standing water. Rather than engineer massive berms, or focus all their energy on draining their property after every rain, we worked *with* the quirks of their property, capturing that water in large shallow pools and planting rice. Aside from planting rice, the pools are also perfect for mud-loving catfish, which became their second income stream associated with the property.

As you look for cash crops that have the possibility of generating enough income to justify the time and energy you will invest in them, consider this: Growing a cash crop is hugely time consuming and competitive, so find a crop that is valued for something more than taste, and that condenses a lot of value into a small amount of product. Americans are getting more adventurous with their diets *and* more health conscious. You can charge a premium for organically grown foods that are high in antioxidants or other healthful qualities. Organic goji berries are full of antioxidants and vitamins and have anti-inflammatory qualities. They thrive in hardiness zones 5 through 9 and currently sell for fifteen dollars per pound (dried), making them a viable crop option for large areas of the country. They can also be sold by mail once dehydrated. Microgreens are quicker to grow and harvest than fully grown leafy greens and are valued for their intense nutrients and antioxidants. Raw goat's milk can work as a crop if you can establish a local network of buyers who will reliably purchase your product. Likewise, organic eggs are a valuable crop to barter or sell locally. Again, you will have to decide if the work of growing and selling is worth the rewards. However, at the very least, having an organic, homegrown crop to barter with your neighbors is always useful.

Sunchokes are perennial tubers that grow prolifically and need relatively little care and attention. They are becoming more popular due to their high quantity of inulin, a type of soluble fiber that supports the all-important gut biome and helps stabilize sugar levels for diabetics. Sunchokes can be juiced, and the resulting liquid boiled down to a sugar substitute syrup. Bear in mind that sunchokes will spread exponentially, and even a small broken-off piece of tuber will take root. You will need to monitor their patch and ensure they don't spread into other areas of your garden: People cannot live on sunchokes alone.

Finally, whatever you grow and however you sell it, make sure you do your research about permits, rules, and regulations. There are plenty of them, and the last thing you want is to fall short of your local boards and ordinances. This is especially relevant if you are mailing or shipping products. So get reading, calling, and talking to find out how to sell your crops safely within the long arms of the law.

THE ROOT CELLAR, OR HOMESTEAD REFRIGERATION

What do Laura Ingalls Wilder (*Little House on the Prairie*) and a refrigerator have in common? Nothing. What do Laura Ingalls Wilder and refrigeration have in common? Everything. This turn of the century homesteader/author (she and her husband, Almanzo, began their homesteading life together in the late 1890s) actually wrote extensively about growing food and preserving that food in a cool, humid root cellar.

For centuries, root cellars played a crucial role in keeping families fed over the span of a long, cold winter. Then someone invented the refrigerator, and that (as they say) was that. Or was it? Today, as more and more people seek some semblance of self-sufficiency, we've seen a resurgence of gardens and greenhouses "sprouting" up across America. And it seems Laura's (off-grid) way of preserving those homegrown vegetables and canned foods is making a comeback. If you've never heard of a root cellar, or only distantly remember it as something your grandparents might have had, I'm here to tell you that a root cellar can make you more food, more energy, and more worst-case-scenario resilient. In fact, root cellars are an easy way to dramatically improve the viability of your homestead, especially if the power ever goes off for a long period of time.

To refrigerate something is to subject it to cold temperatures. The optimum (cold) temperature of a root cellar should hover between 34 to 45 degrees Fahrenheit. But what exactly is a root cellar? Think of a structure built into the ground (or bank) designed to capture the naturally cool temperatures of the earth, which becomes cooler the deeper you dig.

We dug out a root cellar in Fairbanks, Alaska, which is less than two hundred miles from the Arctic Circle, during the month of February. Every morning the temperature hovered around zero with a steady 10 mph breeze. According to the wind chill chart, that was 16 below zero. Brutal. We also built one in Grand Junction, Colorado, during the balmy summer month of June. When finished, each was about twelve feet into the side of a sloping bank, and both worked well for Alaska and Colorado, respectively. It's fairly simple to achieve these cooler root cellar temperatures in Alaska, for obvious (said) reasons. And the Colorado root cellar (earth) wasn't quite as cold as the Alaska root cellar. This tells you that the farther south you go, the more challenging a "working" root cellar becomes.

What is a "working" root cellar? A working root cellar will preserve vegetables that have roots, such as carrots, radishes, turnips, beets, rutabagas, potatoes, and so on. Add to the (rooted) vegetable list fruits, nuts, corn, canned goods, or anything you want to keep cool. You southerners are a long way from Colorado and Alaska, and your ambient temperatures are much higher. Guess what? So are your southern ground temperatures. It may not be worth your time and effort to build a root cellar, especially if you're far south enough to actually grow food year-round. But food can perish, and that's why 129 million households in America own at least one refrigerator. Worldwide, 200 million refrigerators are sold each year. The carbon footprint to fabricate and power these appliances is staggering. In fact, even a nonworking refrigerator is a potential threat to the environment as it can leak chlorofluorocarbons (dangerous chemicals), causing injury to humans (heart, liver, kidneys) and damage to the ozone layer. Not cool. But root cellars actually help you minimize your carbon footprint. And that's . . . pretty cool.

Many people say a root cellar should be at least ten feet deep, because at that depth you'll find optimum cool temperatures. That's a deep hole, and how do you get down there? I recommend digging into the side of a bank, creating a "walk-in" root cellar. You can still find those cooler earth temps as you tunnel horizontally into the bank about the same distance, ten feet. Whether it be concrete blocks, logs, framing materials, steel, or an upcycled tank, dirt is heavy, and you want this thing (especially the roof) to be bombproof. And speaking of bombproof, those of you in tornado alley may want your root cellar to serve a dual purpose, and to use it as a storm shelter as well. This does require a door design meeting the actual specs to withstand a tornado (and those specs exist).

More important than blurting out "a root cellar must be ten feet deep" is learning how deep the frost line is in your area. If you live in an area where the ground freezes in winter, find out how far down it can freeze. One foot? Two feet? Four feet? I wanted to know the frost line of Missouri, and discovered it is thirty to thirty-six inches. Why the curiosity? A fifteen-year-old Laura Ingalls fell for a twenty-five-year-old Almanzo Wilder but had to wait until she was eighteen to marry, which she did. The Wilders then paid one hundred dollars for forty acres in Missouri, circa 1890. I've been to that very property three separate times while visiting various homesteaders nearby, and I found it thoroughly impressive. Why? Well, to start with, after working their land, they fittingly named it . . . Rocky Ridge. I've walked all over that homestead and indeed, there's a lot of dark brown rock. In fact, it's been said that the only fight that couple ever had (or perhaps the worst one . . .) was over the big rock fireplace she wanted when they built their first home, and where she wanted that rock to come from.

There's a stream behind their very well-built home, which is lined with a fractured type of stone (not your typical round river rock). It's a bit of a haul from the stream to the house, and it seems ol' Almanzo didn't want a huge masonry fireplace, nor one built out of that (distant) heavy, jagged stone (come on Laura, don't take your husband for . . . granite). But if you visit that homestead in Mansfield, Missouri, today, you will in fact see a massive stone fireplace dominating one side of their home. It's actually quite attractive, professionally crafted, and clad with TONS of rock carried by hand and back, from . . . that distant stream. And check this out: Years prior (in 1888), they both contracted diphtheria, which resulted in Almanzo walking with a limp the rest of his life. And along with that limp he developed some breathing problems. Yet in spite of all these serious physical setbacks, he also dug a root cellar in this very rocky terrain so that his family could get through the Missouri winters. How deep did he dig it? My guess is he went thirty-six inches, down to the frost line. This formula ensured his produce would not freeze, should they have an unusually cold winter.

Today (because your life probably doesn't depend on it, like it did for earlier homesteaders), a root cellar can be as simple as burying a metal garbage can flush with the ground. Just drill some holes in the bottom to allow the cool air in and drill a hole in the lid to let any warm air escape. I'd definitely have an insulated lid over the whole thing, but that simple design will actually preserve some vegetables like potatoes. Most likely, though, you're wanting a walk-in root cellar. The best universal example I can think of starts with a box six feet square. Excavate an area at the edge of a bank, and build the box right there. Hopefully the bank you've chosen is facing north, as you're looking for every single advantage to keep this thing cool (south-facing walls/doors/windows get way more sun and heat). Frame the walls out of 2' by 8's and the roof out of 2' by 12's. Lay everything out on one-foot centers and then sheet it with 3/4" plywood. Obviously your one north-facing wall is your access door, so now you're looking at what resembles a big doghouse.

Your next step is ventilation. Don't overthink this simple but critical step. Vegetables give off ethylene gas, and those vegetable gases combined with stale air (from an unvented, damp hole in the ground) make for a pungent greeting when you open your root cellar door. To prevent those musty odors from ever getting started, you'll need to create some type of air movement. How? Buy two pieces of 4" PVC plastic pipe, each 10' long. Drill a four-inch hole in the far left side of your box on the top. Drop in one 10' piece from the top and let it get to twelve inches from the bottom of your box. Secure that pipe with screws, glue, or anything to keep it stationary, but make sure it's twelve inches from the bottom of the root cellar floor when finished. Next, drill a four-inch hole on top of the far right side of your box. Cut the second 10' plastic pipe in half, and drop a few inches of this five-foot length in from the top and secure it in place. At this point you have created a cold air intake, drawing fresh outside air in from the left. The far right plastic pipe vent allows fresh air to escape (like smoke going out a chimney), taking with it any significant odors. Your two simple vents actually create air movement. Intake is on the left bottom, outtake is on the right top. A constant flow of fresh air is "breathed in" and "exhaled," perpetually.

At this point in the build, cover the entire structure with two layers of 6 mil plastic or one layer of Bituthene. I don't care what you cover it with (rubber roofing?), but if you choose not to do any waterproofing, it may start dripping on all your produce, which is unsanitary and annoying. Once you're convinced that all water will run down the sides (and into the ground), it's time to cover every square inch of this box with two-inch-thick blue board insulation (this sells for around a dollar per square foot; a 4′ by 8′ sheet costs $32). Listen: We're trying to keep the cold in. Lastly, cover it with at least three feet of dirt.

Remember that five-foot-long "chimney vent"? You're going to carefully backfill dirt over the top of your "box" and around this vertical pipe. Make sure the two 4″ pipes have a 90-degree elbow on the top to prevent rain from entering the root cellar. In fact, you can add another 90-degree elbow to the first one, making the vertical vent actually point straight down. Add some type of fine mesh inside the pipe to prevent insects from entering. Once you've backfilled the entire build right up to the sides of the door, you will no longer be looking at a box. You will be looking at a root cellar. Most likely you will want one a bit larger. No worries. Just remember dirt is heavy and we don't want a cave-in at the ol' mine-shaft. If you want to go bigger, perhaps make it deeper into the bank (tapping into cooler soil) but minimize the width, as the wider span increases the bearing load of whatever your structural roofing is.

Make sure the door is super insulated, as this is now your weakest link. In fact, adding a little enclosed hallway and adding another front door is a very novel idea. It allows less refrigerated air to escape. Example: You go in through the first door and close it behind you before you actually open up the root cellar main door. Obviously, you do the same on the way out. It definitely keeps the cold air contained in the root cellar, and the "breezeway" itself remains cool. All of this effort pays off in . . . fresh vegetables.

I've built this system before and I highly recommend everyone copy this design. Feel free to steal it, and don't worry, there is no copyright in"fridge"ment.

What does Laura Ingalls Wilder have in common with every homesteader I've ever met (besides wanting a working root cellar . . .)? Perseverance. The Wilders faced crop failures, natural disasters, the loss of a son, diphtheria, and a house fire that burned every single thing that they owned. They took second, and third, jobs to support their homestead. They sold eggs, took in boarders, worked in the apple orchard, delivered kerosene, and all the while never gave up on their forty-acre homestead dream. What would be the last words she would ever write as an author and homesteader? "It is a beautiful world." Amen.

ELEVEN

LIVESTOCK

A homestead isn't a homestead without livestock—perhaps. Even the most committed vegan needs animals on his or her property. Livestock are an essential part of the regenerative agriculture practices that most homesteaders—knowingly or not—are following. You may have zero interest in eating chickens *or* eggs. But you are going to need those chickens turning over and scratching your fallow land, eating caterpillars, grubs, and other insects, and laying down a rich layer of fertilizer for next year's harvest (you'll want to protect your vegetables and greens from the chickens, however). Likewise, guinea fowl. Even if they aren't valuable as meat animals, they pay their own keep in tick removal and as "watch birds," letting you know when predators—or people—get too close to your property. Goats are invaluable for clearing dense brambles and invasive species from your land (they really come into their own when you need to thin out or clear a fire break from around your property). Turkeys are smarter than chickens and don't have a constant need to scratch. As a result, they are cleaner and don't make such a mess of their coop. If you choose to raise heritage breeds, like Black Spanish or Bourbon Reds, you can sell the meat at a premium come Thanksgiving.

Livestock also gives you an opportunity for a revenue source right on your property. Your meat, eggs, and milk will be organic, free-range, and highly desirable. When you first start out, you may be limited to bartering your goods rather than directly selling them, but eventually, as you refine your homesteading skills and learn what works and what doesn't, you will have a reliable and predictable source of income. Here's something else to consider: As Americans' tastes in food grow more expansive and international, more and more animals will become viable meat crops. Likewise, as more Americans start to understand and embrace eating organic, free-range food (think of the explosion of interest in grass-fed beef), you'll have an opportunity to sell to more health-conscious folks as well. Those homesteaders in Louisiana now have a hybrid rice paddy/catfish pond. We helped another family in Alaska set up a commercial kitchen to process their salmon catch. Find a meat product that will thrive in your particular terrain and be open to the unexpected: Emus are raised both for their low-cholesterol, heart-healthy meat *and* for the 2.5 gallons of oil extracted from their fat. Alpacas are raised for the five to eight pounds of valuable fiber they grow each year. Get creative, and think outside the box to find a livestock animal that will thrive in your particular conditions.

All livestock have pros and cons. Your main job is to give them a safe and contained environment, give them good feed, and be attentive to signs of ill health or disease. It's also critical to differentiate between pets and livestock. The minute you give a pig a name, it's a pet. Processing animals isn't easy for a newbie homesteader, but it's *easier* if you know in your heart that you gave them a good life, and you were able to dispatch them quickly and painlessly. Let's look at the five most common livestock species, and what you need to do to house, care for, and process them cleanly.

CHICKENS

Nothing says homestead more than a flock of chickens. Nothing says *Homestead Rescue* more than a flock of chickens that are slowly being picked off by coyotes, raptors, or other predators. I've lost count of the number of homesteads we've visited where the chickens were underhoused or, worse, fully free-range: nice in principle, terrible in practice.

Nonhomesteaders tend to think of a generic "chicken" when they contemplate establishing a coop. There is a bit more that you need to know. Chickens are generally divided into egg-layers and bigger meat birds (although some birds meet both needs). Egg-laying chickens can be harvested and processed when they age out of laying, but the bird will be smaller and the meat will be tougher. Within the egg-laying category there are multiple different types of birds. Before you order your chicks (and yes, they are delivered by USPS, cheeping and peeping all the way), consider the characteristics that will give your flock the best chance of success. Will they need to survive tough winters? Pick a species with fluffy, insulated feathers such as the Orpington, or a species with a smaller peacomb (the rough, unfeathered flesh that hangs down below their beak) such as the Ameraucana (also known as "Easter Eggers" because of their bright blue and green eggs). The smaller exposed area will leave them less susceptible to frostbite. Andalusians are heat-resistant, will keep laying even in high temperatures, and are the proverbial "tough bird." Bantams lay smaller eggs and require less feed.

Some smaller, lighter species of egg-laying birds like the Ameraucana are considered "flighty" and are able to fly short distances to roost in trees or evade predators (this isn't an issue with heavier species such as the Orpington). Flightiness isn't necessarily a problem, as most chickens will instinctively return to their coop at the end of the day. These birds forage more, meaning they require less feed. Homesteaders are divided about whether the bird's flightiness puts them more or less at risk of predation. They are naturally curious and like to explore, exposing them to eagles, hawks, or other avian predators; however, they are better able to evade ground dwellers like raccoons or other rodents. So, bear that in mind if you buy species like the Ameraucana.

It's important to understand how your environment will affect the birds. Our rooster (Nubs) is a large bird, but he has no toes because his first owners gave him (and the other chickens) a conventional rail perch that they could grip with their claws. In the extreme cold of an Alaska winter, those exposed claws froze, and the birds lost their toes. Not great for them, but luckily they found a new owner in Mollee, who did some research and found out that Alaskan chickens (or any extreme cold-weather chickens) need flat planks to sit on at night. Their feet are protected by their body heat and their toes stay intact. Chickens likewise need help dealing with heat—always make sure they have enough fresh water and shade to rest in.

Our chickens are Rhode Island Reds. Over the winter we turn off the lights in the coop, which encourages the birds to go dormant and stop laying. No particular reason other than they work hard and should get a little time off too (as of this past November, our "dormant" chickens are still giving four eggs per day).

The Cornish Cross is the undisputed champ of meat birds because of its docile, passive temperament and ability to put on large amounts of weight in a short amount of time. They don't forage and they eat a huge amount of feed, but they are ready for harvest in a quarter of the time of other birds. Young birds (known as Cornish game hens) can be harvested at four weeks old. At six weeks they are essentially an adult size. Their meat has a lot of fat, making it delicious to eat, but the birds occasionally overeat to the point where they break their own legs. Red Rangers are popular with regenerative agriculture practitioners because they forage extensively and have lively personalities. Meat birds are generally more sensitive to the cold than egg-layers, so bear that in mind.

POULTRY IN MOTION

Which leads us to our next point: the chicken coop or tractor. Before you buy your first chick or poult, you need to construct a predator-proof coop and chicken run. It is possible to let your chickens out to roam while you are supervising them, but realistically most homesteaders don't have the time to be fully attentive to or protective of a flock of chickens wandering their property. So, find a spot on your property that is close to your house, that has adequate sun and shade, and that you can easily keep an eye on as you go about your day.

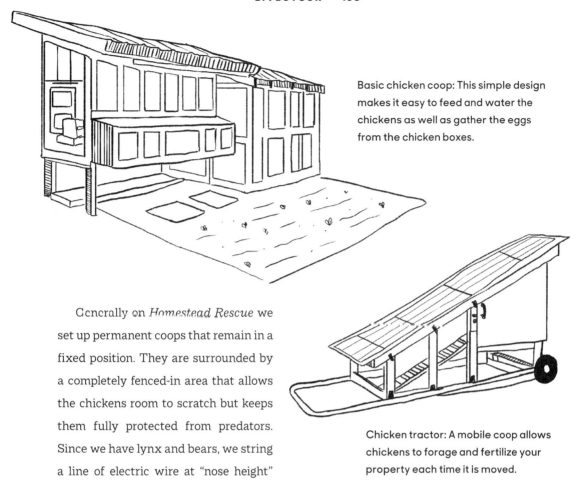

Basic chicken coop: This simple design makes it easy to feed and water the chickens as well as gather the eggs from the chicken boxes.

Chicken tractor: A mobile coop allows chickens to forage and fertilize your property each time it is moved.

Generally on *Homestead Rescue* we set up permanent coops that remain in a fixed position. They are surrounded by a completely fenced-in area that allows the chickens room to scratch but keeps them fully protected from predators. Since we have lynx and bears, we string a line of electric wire at "nose height" around the coop to discourage predators. Our dog, Little Su, has touched it once; never again. She howled like she had been hit by lightning. (FYI: Electric fences range between 2,000 and 10,000 volts. Lightning bolts range from 300 million to a billion volts.) Birds need access to fresh grass and they do help with pests and weeds, so let them roam if you know you are going to be working in the immediate area, and lure them back into their coop with grain once you have to leave.

The other option is a lighter-weight chicken tractor, where the coop is built on wheels and is easily moved from one area to another. Often there is a fenced-in area protected by an electric fence fed by solar power. This allows your chickens to scratch over a larger area of your property, fertilizing it and breaking up the topsoil. The disadvantage of this style of chicken tractor is that there is no overhead protection from raptors, and moving it requires time and energy and attention that the homesteader might not have to spare. Predators are well aware of your chickens—and the electric fence. The one evening you forget to turn the electric fence back on after collecting eggs or checking on the flock will be the night that they get in and wreak havoc on your birds. Not only will they kill multiple birds and severely injure others, but the surviving hens will be in shock afterward, and it may be weeks before they get back to laying regularly. Frankly, we've heard too many stories of chickens that have met bad ends while supposedly being protected by these kinds of moveable electric fences, so our first choice is often a fixed coop. Dave (the Smartest Homesteader I Know) built his own fully enclosed chicken tractor, shaped like a piece of pie sitting on its side. Every so often he moves it a few feet, allowing his chickens to peck and scratch all over his yard.

There are dozens of prefabricated coops out there, easily available online and delivered overnight to be set up in your yard. Building your own coop out of lumber and chicken wire is a few days' project. *But* I can almost guarantee you that somewhere on your property or in the local area you have something that can—with a little creativity and deep cleaning—serve as a coop that is just as good as or better than anything you can order online, and will take less time and money to prepare than building one from scratch. In Season Eight of *Homestead Rescue* we made a chicken/turkey coop out of a wooden boat that had been in dry dock for decades. The shipyard owner was so thrilled to off-load this unseaworthy item that he sold it to the homesteaders for twenty-five dollars. Misty stripped it down, removing the interior structure, the cabin, and all the electronics, added in flooring, and built up a high roof structure to replace the old cabin. She salvaged old storage boxes originally used to hold fishing tackle and turned them into laying boxes. The boat was large enough to accommodate both chickens and turkeys in two separate living areas, and, most important, was still sturdy enough to be completely predator-proof (an issue, since ermines had killed the last flock). Another homesteader converted an old playhouse into a coop, and a third homesteader did the same with his kids' old treehouse.

So before you set aside time to build up a chicken coop from scratch, look on your property, look at Craigslist, and look around your local area for a small existing structure that can be repurposed. Understand the particular needs of your location and adjust your design to reflect them. As Misty showed with the boat, it pays to be creative. So long as the structure is mold-free, sturdy, and has no rot or other issues, it's a candidate for getting a second lease on life as a coop. What's more, with a little paint and a creative eye, these old structures can add to the aesthetic charm of your homestead. That old playhouse was painted red to match the barns already on the property. Now, instead of adding stress to the homesteader's life, the chickens—and their little red barn—add eggs, eventually meat, and a lot of joy to the homestead.

GUINEA FOWL AND TURKEYS

Chickens aren't the only poultry in town. Guinea fowl are small birds, weighing about three pounds each, that originally came from Africa. They are becoming increasingly popular with homesteaders because they are superb free-range birds—although they don't really fly, they are fast, crafty runners, evading predators and snatching up insects, and even small snakes and vermin. If you have a tick problem, they can help suction up these very problematic pests without being affected by the diseases they carry. Their small eggs are delicious, and guinea fowl meat is often considered better than chicken. What's the downside? They are LOUD. Guinea fowl will alert you to any man or beast setting foot on your property. If you are within shouting distance of your neighbors, you'll probably be hearing *their* thoughts about *your* birds—perhaps at three a.m. after the local coyote comes a-sniffing around the guinea fowl coop. Personally, I'm all in favor of animals that alert you to *other* animals. But they may not be a good choice for you if keeping the noise down is an issue.

Turkeys, especially heritage breeds like the Narragansett, Royal Palm, or Standard Bronze, among many others, are becoming more popular. Turkeys are generally calmer than chickens and lay large eggs that can be sold just like chicken eggs.

PIGS

Once you have successfully kept poultry and perhaps goats, you can consider keeping pigs. They are easygoing and friendly, love to forage and uproot invasive brambles and other plants, and turn over your topsoil. Their manure will fertilize and revitalize your property. But . . . unlike poultry or goats, pigs have one purpose on a homestead. There is no milk or eggs to justify their presence. At some point you will have to

Berkshire pigs: Pigs require adequate fencing (strong). Skip this step and you have pigdemonium.

dispatch and process the animals. If you've kept more than one pig, you'll have seen that they form affectionate bonds with each other and with you. If you've kept them well, the pigs will trust you, and show their trust by ambling up to you and greeting you when you check on them. Pigs are believed to be as smart as dogs, and they have similarly rich and visible emotional lives as canines. We worked with a family in an early episode who were raising hogs, theoretically to sell. However, they were so emotionally attached to them they had been unable to process any of the animals.

If you decide that you are up to the challenge of keeping pigs, there are two ways to go. Berkshire pigs are the king of pastured pork and can grow to be six hundred pounds. They have to reach at least that size for the meat to become fully marbled. Although they forage, you will be feeding them pig feed for most of their adult life (despite the popular myth, pigs cannot survive or thrive on slops). This adds up, so make sure you run the numbers on how much feed you are going to be buying before you purchase your piglets. Processing these animals is hard work, requiring at least two and possibly three people. Smaller breeds, like the New Zealand Kunekune, grow to about half the size of the Berkshire and are easier to process and handle.

Pigs are sensitive creatures: Industrial pigs suffer from a lack of play and socialization, eventually chewing off other pigs' tails out of boredom and anxiety. Homestead pigs will need a warm, safe place at night, a shaded area during the hot days, and plenty of water and mud for wallowing. They will need an elevated trough for their feed (placing feed on the ground will ensure that most of it gets trodden into the mud) and a clean source of water for drinking. In areas with bears or cougars you'll need to make sure that their sleeping area is secure enough to repel these large predators.

When it is time to process the pigs, find a local mentor who will help you through the process. You can most likely barter a share of the meat for this person's time and knowledge.

One final observation: Pigs and chickens go well together. Pigs tend to wolf down their feed, meaning that their feces are full of undigested seeds and grains. The chickens will peck and forage through the manure, quickly breaking it down and helping it to integrate into the soil.

GOATS

Goats are truly all-purpose livestock, with four direct revenue sources—fiber, meat, kids, and milk—and one indirect revenue source: bramble and invasive weed clearing. And believe it or not, I know some moose hunters in Alaska who have used goats to pack out the hundreds of pounds of meat (and also pull carts and plows). A Saanen dairy goat can be milked year-round and will give 2.5 to 3 gallons of milk a day. Raw goat's milk can be sold for up to ten to twelve dollars a gallon (check to see rules and regulations for selling raw milk in your area), meaning that you have a consistent source of income from the animals all year. Raw goat's milk is becoming increasingly popular because of the belief that it retains beneficial elements like amino acids, antimicrobials, fatty acids, and minerals and vitamins that are destroyed when milk is pasteurized. If raw milk is outlawed in your area, you may have to use a barter system rather than offering it directly for sale.

Goats are relatively low maintenance *except* for their ability to escape pens, jump over fences, and generally cause havoc if they get out. Make sure that you use the proper fencing on a goat pen. No fencing with squares larger than 4″ by 4″ should be used. A fence with 6″ by 6″ squares allows a goat's horns to get stuck in the fence. Kids are charming and delightful and will entrance and entertain your children—and probably you too.

Finally, ten goats can clear an acre of land in about a month. More goats = faster time. If you are living in an area where brush poses a fire risk, a herd of goats can earn their keep by clearing that land and eventually being leased out to other homeowners to clear their land. Goats can clear steep hillsides (which are inherently more dangerous in a fire) or rocky hillsides. They have no problems clearing out steep gorges (which also funnel and intensify fire) or other landscapes that human beings can't safely reach. All in all, goats can add to your homestead in multiple ways . . . and that's hard to "bleat."

TWELVE

HUNTING

I've heard that "vegan" was actually an old Native American word that meant (when translated) "bad hunter." But if you are not vegan (defined by its more common definition), you may find an organic, healthy, protein-rich food source is literally at your fingertips, or trigger fingertip, that is. A subsistence lifestyle often includes harvesting your own wild game, from free-ranging turkeys to moose. And speaking of moose, I had moose tacos last night at the cabin with freshly harvested homestead potatoes and veggies. Epic. Moose, caribou, Dall sheep (and mountain goats), and lots of salmon have supplemented our garden and greenhouse table settings for nearly fifty years in Alaska. It doesn't take much research before you become wary of the meat sold at your local market.

Chicken, pork, and beef have "processed" derivatives that have been proven harmful to humans (for example, lunch meats). Did you know moose have one percent (or less) fat? Compare that to 35 to 55 percent fat in store-bought poultry, pork, and beef. Moose is high in potassium, low in sodium, and has a long list of vitamin and mineral benefits. And, at 100 calories per 100 gram serving, it is the original lean cuisine. Bear in mind that you will need some fat in your diet in order to digest protein. A strange thought, I know: Most on-grid people have to worry about getting *too much* fat, but if you are truly off-grid, you may have the opposite problem and find yourself with too *little* fat. We need fat in order to fully digest protein, which is why extreme survivalists prize fatty beaver, bear, or porcupine meat (some old-timers still refer to protein poisoning as rabbit starvation or caribou sickness). It's a balance.

Caribou can be eaten raw, frozen, aged, dried, smoked, or roasted. Like moose, it too is high in vitamins and minerals and weighs in at 130 calories per 100 gram serving. Both animals eat organically, and neither has ever dined on processed feed or been injected with steroids or antibiotics to make them grow faster and bigger. Also, don't think for a second there's anything humane in the commercial (crowded, confined, killing) raising and processing of poultry, pork, or beef. Fifty billion chickens per year are slaughtered for food, 750 million of those for KFC alone. Add to that number of slaughtered animals 1.5 billion pigs and 300 million cattle per year. When you choose to grow or raise your own food, you begin to appreciate the health, lifestyle, and moral benefits of all living things organic.

Here's the twist: Despite what you might think, I personally do not like to kill . . . anything. I spotted a moose sporting a record-size antler rack stretching 74½ inches in width, but I went to get my son to stalk and shoot that once-in-a-lifetime kill. My son

Miles took it down with one shot. I had no desire to pull the trigger and frankly have no desire to have bragging rights after a hunt. But I did dive right in to process this majestic moose into four quarters (and change) and pack it back to camp. We are meat hunters, rather than trophy hunters, so those impressive antlers now grace the front of someone else's cabin.

There are 200,000 moose and 750,000 caribou in Alaska, with only 7,000 moose being harvested annually. These two species have allowed native people to survive for centuries in this harsh land known as Alaska. And today, we too choose to "live off the land" as Alaska still is quite bountiful in moose, caribou, and salmon populations. I see it as a humbling privilege to live in a place where you can make your own choice as to what ends up on your dinner table. Again, where did this fast-food chicken sandwich come from? What's the origin of this (whopping . . .) drive-thru burger? Every moose, caribou, Dall sheep, or mountain goat that we've ever taken was standing in a pristine wilderness setting, eating healthy, organic willows, lichen, or assorted wild grasses. They were not crowded en masse, stressed, or treated inhumanely. Hunting is not for everyone, but it is a way of life for many Alaskans leading a subsistence lifestyle.

Most homesteaders in the Lower 48 will be hunting deer or elk as their source of alternative organic protein. Whatever the wild game, treat them all with the reverence they deserve. They each command our respect as they have long played their role (successfully) in the delicate balancing act of survival of the fittest. And whether you believe in creation or evolution, animals were here first. Sadly, hundreds of species are not "here" anymore due to mortal man's dominant, planet-encompassing footprint. Have people learned their lesson? Today's headlines read, "Humans Are Driving One Million Species to Extinction." These words, these facts sadden me.

I am not a sport hunter, but in my quest to live an off-grid, self-sufficient, subsistence lifestyle in Alaska, I've accepted the fact that hunting has been a long-time, inseparable part of living this lifestyle. As we go into winter, our freezer is full of moose and salmon. For that, and to them, I am truly thankful.

My son Miles Raney is the most proficient hunter I know. He pulled the trigger (once) on that 74½-inch monster bull moose. He also harvested a 42-inch Dall sheep. Both are once-in-a-lifetime hunts, but neither of those racks hang on his simple yurt. He hunted old school . . . on foot. No airplanes, no off-road vehicles. And, after it all, no social media posts.

And, for whatever reasons, he no longer hunts, but now lives an Alaskan off-grid lifestyle as a vegan . . . in the common definition.

THE HOMESTEAD HUNTER

Many episodes of *Homestead Rescue* include a Hunting 101 course, taught by my son Matt. These homesteaders—especially if they have migrated to rural living from the big city—are not always schooled in that area. Often our families struggle with the idea of hunting and killing an animal. Understandable, if it's outside of your experience. But part of being a homesteader is taking on the responsibility of doing your part to tend to and care for the land on which you are living, and all the creatures who live there. If there are too many moose it is bad for all moose, because there isn't enough food to go around. Too many bears, same thing. If there were no human beings in the world and these animals were left to Mother Nature to find a balance, great, but that's not the case. Even with the best of intentions we are limiting these animals' habitat, and their opportunities to thrive and survive. It is actually better to hunt these animals than to not.

Think of guns as tools that serve a useful purpose, and that need the same thoughtfulness and care as any other tool on your homestead. So, approach hunting as you approach any other task on your homestead: a skill that you must apprentice in, and take seriously, in order to properly care for the land and the people you love.

For the most part the hunting community understands that *more people* is a good thing (there are always exceptions to this rule, of course). The more people who adopt a subsistence-hunting lifestyle, the more likely it is that land will be preserved and left undeveloped, that animal herds will be managed and culled responsibly, and that hunting will continue to be viewed as a positive thing to be supported and promoted by the local community. Whether you're involved or not, someone is going to hunt those animals. Park service people will get those cull numbers, with or without you. So you can either take advantage of this fact or relinquish your share of the best meat money can('t) buy.

Your very first step is taking a hunter safety course. For most states this is nonnegotiable (there are some exceptions for older hunters; check your state regulations). You will have to show evidence that you took the course in order to apply for and get a tag to hunt whatever animal you have "in your sights." You will learn the basics of how to operate your gun, your crossbow, or other weapon safely and how to stay safe around other hunters when you are in the woods or in other areas of limited visibility. Alaska doesn't require hunter's orange, but it's a good idea to wear it anyway. Once you have passed the course, you can apply for a tag. These tags fund the conservation of the area in which you are hunting. Depending on what you are hoping to hunt, you may have to enter a tag lottery. Finally: Don't be tempted to hunt illegally. It's wrong, and it will open you up to a world of expensive and unpleasant consequences if you are caught. Generally, deer and wild boar tags are easy tags to get. Elk, moose, bison, bighorn sheep, Dall sheep, and a few other big game may be harder to get depending on the state you're hunting in.

Look around for "that guy" who will share his knowledge and might even be open to mentoring you, perhaps in exchange for a portion of whatever you successfully hunt (or your assistance in processing his kill). Join the local shooting range or gun club if you are struggling to find a mentor. Talk. Ask for help. Hire a guide for a day. There are, bare minimum, fifteen million people out there who have the knowledge you need. So keep asking until you find someone willing to share it.

> ## Talk. Ask for help. Hire a guide for a day.

CALIBER

A .22 rifle is the obvious choice for a hunting newcomer. It doesn't really matter who makes it, though all hunters have their favored manufacturers. Matt and I both have taken gun safety courses required by TV production companies (we passed, and they asked us to become instructors), and the .22 caliber rifle is the entry-level firearm of choice. A .22 is an easy gun to shoot (some hunters will refer to it as the "method of take"), and you can get all kinds of game with it. If you're not ready to shoot a larger animal, you can start with upland birds (these are birds such as partridges, grouse, and ptarmigan that live on the land—as opposed to the water—in areas with ground cover). Successfully hunting and harvesting one of these birds is a big moment, and one that will help you change your mindset and get you ready to hunt a larger animal, should you want to. When the time comes to shoot a heavier-caliber round, the experience will feel more comfortable and won't be as jarring.

Guns are also useful as protection against predators. A 12-gauge is the most versatile because you can load it up with so many types of rounds: Even a blank will deter a mountain lion. You can load it with BB shot for a nonlethal defensive shot, or you can load it with shells that will bring down a grizzly bear.

Hunting is not that difficult, *but* you can't do it all at once. The hardest thing is just starting. Even if you simply buy a .22 and learn how to shoot it, this alone would be a huge win, and you'd be miles ahead of someone who doesn't have that experience. Start slow, pick up skills as you feel comfortable. It may be that *you* aren't the person on the homestead most comfortable or excited to hunt. In which case, find the person who is, and let them take over the responsibility for hunting, butchering, and/or preserving the kill.

HUNTING ETIQUETTE

For me, hunting serves two purposes: It feeds my family, and it helps me get even deeper into the wilderness, closer to the animals I love, and farther away from the stress and anxiety of the modern world. I don't use a plane to fly to remote locations or use boats or off-road rigs when hunting. My family does not do "sport" or "trophy" hunting. I'm a decent shot, but I've never taken a shot over two hundred yards, even though plenty of hunters boast of taking shots at five hundred yards or even more. The reason is simple: I'm not completely sure I could cleanly shoot and kill an animal at anything over two hundred, so taking a shot where there's a reasonable chance I will wound an animal rather than kill it is a no-go. Once a year I'll go to "moose camp" with a small group of men I've known for years. We'll usually harvest a few moose and split the meat. For the most part, however, when I go out hunting, I'm with my kids and on foot, setting up a hunting camp for a few nights and striking out early in the morning—before the sun is up—to track our prey.

If you are going to hunt, you have to hunt with respect for the animals, the natural world, and the other humans you might see (or more problematically, not see) out there. Part of this respect is fully processing the kill, and butchering and packing out all the meat you can from the carcass. There are a lot of hunters who are far less interested in the hard, dirty work of butchering than they are in seeking trophies for stories to share in the coming days. Not cool, and frankly you are missing the point if you leave meat behind when you walk out of the wilderness. Look at the regulations. It's illegal and called "wanton waste." My son Miles, the vegan, will skin and butcher a moose or caribou until the carcass is white. Every muscle or organ is gone, loaded up in our backpacks or however we are packing it out. So, be a serious hunter. Understand harvesting animals is a privilege, and treat those animals with respect and decency.

— THIRTEEN —

PREDATORS

I've been chased by a grizzly in Denali:
You'd be surprised how fast you can run when
you are being chased by a bear

WOLVES ON THE FORTY

Everywhere we go in the country, homesteaders are losing sheep, chickens, goats, and other small animals to predators (most commonly coyotes). Now, when it comes to predators, I've come face to face with many. I've been chased by grizzlies, charged by moose, and stalked by black bears and cougars (when I lived in the Cascade Mountains of Washington State). Once I called in a pack of five wolves, and we can often hear coyotes from our bedroom window. We even have resident wolverines. In short: We have predators. Every single predator on the earth—or at least in Hatcher Pass—has checked out our chicken coop (and we haven't had a loss yet, thanks to Mollee's single line of electric wire that runs at snout height around the coop).

I don't feel that the animals that live in our radius are predators. I consider them neighbors. And, as a neighbor, I like to think I am in tune with the local events. However, when it comes to the wilderness and all of the predators that live there, I'm constantly aware of my place in this pecking order. Right now it's been a few days since I've walked the property, and I am aware that I'm *less* in tune with what's happening on our patch than I normally would be.

Four years ago, out hiking in Hatcher Pass, I ran across a yearling moose (fresh) kill, right on the game trail that we use to climb the mountain for recreation. The kill was so recent that there was fresh blood pooled up in the rib cage. Whatever killed this thing was close. I wasn't afraid, but I definitely realized the potential danger of this moose kill right next to our family hiking trail. I told all my family members of the location, and for the next few months I checked in on the kill every so often, expecting to see it covered in a huge pile of tundra, dirt, and sticks, which would be typical of a brown bear protecting its kill. But this never happened. I think the moose was small enough that coyotes and wolves made quick work of it, and it wasn't worth a bear's interest to go to the effort of claiming and burying what little was left.

Then, next winter, the wolves killed a much larger two-year-old moose. Now they had my attention: I put up a game camera and caught wolves, ermine, owls, and other creatures feeding on the carcass (the bears were in hibernation). I saw two wolves, though I suspected there were at least four. During this period of time, our entire family went on a ski tour, and we all saw a majestic black wolf running across the snow. Epic! Later I saw a gray wolf. Most likely there were more.

There are plenty in Alaska who would take a shot at those wolves, for fun or for profit. But it would never enter my mind to kill one. Why? Because having the experience of watching them up close like this was priceless, and a six-hundred-dollar (or more) pelt paled to disrespectful insignificance compared to this once-in-a-lifetime opportunity. During the next few months these wolves started to get very close to the house. One afternoon, two separate wolves were howling back and forth, communicating about something. I decided to just let nature happen, not to investigate, and not to disturb the wolves. Instead, I listened, and the next day I went for a hike to see what they were up to.

Overnight it snowed five inches, and the next morning I followed their crystal-clear tracks through the fresh snowfall. Indeed, there were two wolves tracking a mama moose and a baby moose. They were clearly communicating back and forth on what maneuvers to make to take down this small moose. I tracked them for a few hundred yards and it looked like the wolves gave up. All of this was happening within a ten-minute walk from my back door, and this is one of the main reasons that I live like this, to be closer to nature.

The next winter after that, very little wolf activity. Did someone look at wolves differently than I do and shoot them? Perhaps. Did they move on to greener pastures, where there was more game? Maybe. Personally I miss them. I spent many days tracking and placing game cameras, and just enjoying being on this mountain knowing the wolves were here somewhere.

Before the wolves left they made overtures to our dog, Little Su. I noticed they were coming very close to the cabin, day or night, and during this time Su, a purebred giant Alaskan malamute (140 pounds), came in heat, and her behavior started to change. Wolves can be very dangerous to dogs: I have a friend in Cantwell, Alaska, who told me how a few years ago a local pack of wolves killed a dog musher's ten sled dogs but spared just the one female sled dog that was in heat.

One afternoon, Su and I were standing in the yard with wolves howling literally a couple hundred yards away. Su just stood there looking into the forest (in heat), never making a sound. No barking, not a whimper. What was she thinking? Clearly she was making plans of some kind, because soon afterward, on a very cold and dark January night, I got a call from a snowmachiner coming out of the pass who had picked up a lost malamute and called the number on her tag. I hurriedly walked down the trail, crossed the river, jumped in my truck, met up with the caller, and retrieved Su. When I got her back to the forty, we crossed the river ice and began the eight-hundred-foot hike up to the cabin, navigating by headlamp in the dark.

But for the first time ever, she stopped on the trail and wouldn't obey. She turned around and headed back for the river, and the road. She wanted to go out for the night. I remember feeling so sad that there was something more important to her than her family (me and Mollee) and the warm cabin. What was out there? I had a pretty good idea what the attraction was.

When the guy told me where he had picked her up, I knew right away she was hanging out at the wolf crossing, about a mile upriver above our cabin. I truly thought that Su would have wolf pups in the spring. Luckily that didn't come to pass, since in Alaska it is illegal to own hybrid wolves, and I knew the state of Alaska would kill them. Still, I had a strong feeling that those wolves came face to face with Little Su on the one and only night, in her four years, that she had gone up into Hatcher Pass without us.

One year later, in early winter, we just got our first three inches of snow. I look forward to this time of year because I can see where the animals are based on their tracks, something I can't do in summer. I saw lynx tracks, close to the cabin and close to the chicken coop (I can't say enough about an electric fence). A few minutes later I ran into a plethora of moose tracks, and on my way home, I turned down a different route, and there they were: one set of fresh wolf tracks. Are they back? I hope so.

———————————

As you develop your homestead you will no doubt hear stories from the locals about the coyotes, bears, cougars, wolves, or bobcats that roam the hills and forests around you. (The day you bring your first chicken or goat on the property, you'll start to hear about them yourself, directly from the source, as word gets around the four-legged carnivore community.) Depending on the person talking, they may speak with reverence, respect, annoyance, or even downright antipathy. But no matter what your neighbors think, it's important that you understand that you are the new kid in town. The predators and prey were getting along fine before you arrived, you're the disruptive force, and you need to be at least somewhat willing to adapt to their way of life, rather than attempt to eradicate the wild animals in your area. It's also important to understand that while we may imagine predators to be large and dangerous animals like grizzlies, the predators that will actually cause you a problem are more likely to be small rodents like ermine, small carnivores like foxes, and omnivores like raccoons.

Adapting to predators means building secure pens for your livestock and protecting your animals (and children) from hungry carnivores. It means understanding your responsibility to maintain your property in a way that actively discourages predators from paying a visit. As mentioned in an earlier chapter: Trash needs to be removed and either burned or trucked to the dump regularly, and compost needs to be covered or otherwise inaccessible to bears, raccoons, or other small predators.

If you have a crawl space under your house, it needs to have—at a minimum—a chicken wire barrier, buried at least a foot in the soil and stapled firmly to the bottom lip of your house. Why? Well, if you've ever lived over a crawl space that has been claimed by a family of omnivorous skunks, you'll understand. (It's quite literally chemical warfare, and can be so caustic to breathe that badly affected rooms become borderline uninhabitable. Not a problem for us, as there are no skunks or snakes in Alaska.) If you hunt, you need to be smart about how and where you process your game. The worst bear attacks happen over game carcasses that a bear has claimed. Many a guide or hunter who's returned to a kill after leaving it overnight has learned this the hard way.

Avoiding or deterring predators is your job, not theirs. If hungry carnivores are coming too close to your property, livestock, or children, that's because you haven't done the work you need to do in making your homestead unappealing or actively repulsive to these animals.

Over the course of the show we've worked with families who have had close encounters with big predators in their area. On a day-to-day basis, though, it's less dramatic predators, like coyotes, foxes, ermine,

> ## Avoiding or deterring predators is your job, not theirs.

and raptors, that cause the biggest problems. These smaller predators aren't always interested in people, but they *are* very interested in the animals that people bring with them.

COYOTES

Some biologists rate coyotes as smarter than wolves. High praise. Although Alaskans would highly disagree (including me), this rating does sing the praises of the wily predator. In the 1700s, coyotes lived squarely in the middle of the country, their range running up from

Mexico, through Western Texas, up through the Great Plains, Colorado, Wyoming, and Montana. As hunters, cowboys, and other new populations began to cull wolves and bears, the coyote population exploded, expanding into new territories as the alpha predator. Today, wily and resilient coyotes live in every state other than Hawaii, and they have comfortably expanded into suburban and even urban landscapes. There are two lessons to take from this: The first is that we need predators, if only to keep other predators in check. The second is that every human action has a *reaction* in the natural world. Those early settlers had a simplistic approach to the animals they viewed as threats: Get rid of them! However, they inadvertently opened up space in the environment around them for a new predator, the coyote. Growing up I never heard stories of coyotes attacking humans, but now, as man and coyote come into more frequent contact, reports of aggressive coyotes are increasing.

> # Every human action has a *reaction* in the natural world.

A coyote behaving "naturally" is shy and skittish, active during dusk and dawn, and rarely seen during the day but occasionally spotted at night. Coyotes who are present but still shy and elusive are not a huge threat, but you will still need to keep pets on that tight leash, and make sure any free-roaming cats are home safe by the evening. These coyotes have never been fed by misguided but well-meaning people. They've never had access to a trash pile or a compost heap. They've never killed a chicken or a cat. Congratulations! Your homestead management skills have successfully deterred a potentially problematic predator.

Unfortunately, many of our homesteaders have not been so successful. Remember when we discussed the importance of a fortified chicken coop? When coyotes gain access to chickens, all bets are off. These coyotes have found an easy and reliable food source and will consider your homestead a KFC drive-thru.

BLACK AND BROWN BEARS

Alaska has one hundred thousand black bears, thirty thousand brown bears, and five thousand polar bears. And just like coyotes, black bears are expanding their territory, are growing in number, and can be found in nearly all fifty states. Most of us think of black bears as relatively benign. Growing up we never worried about running across one (unless it was a sow with cubs), unlike the vastly more dangerous brown bear (or grizzly). These black bears were more of a pest than a threat, breaking into cars to forage for granola bars and tearing down bird feeders to gorge on birdseed. But, like with the coyote, this balance is changing as bears move into suburban settings: A study in Asheville found that most female dens were less than five hundred feet from a residence (male dens were over triple the distance from the nearest house).

Bears will only be a problem if you let them be. Most bears are opportunistic. They are looking for easily available food and aren't picky where they find it. We've all seen images of hungry polar bears foraging in trash piles in the Arctic. Frankly it's a depressing sight, but it goes to show that a hungry bear has no problem eating all types of garbage. It's not the bears' fault: They are exploiting a resource, and will continue to do so as long as the resource is available to them. Your trash needs to be secured and disposed of quickly. If you are regularly seeing bears, make sure you are rinsing out food packaging before you put it in your trash. All of these steps are as good for the bear as they are for you: A bear that associates trash or humans with food is a bear that is going to be shot or euthanized in the near future. (A trash bear is a dead bear.) Anytime you make it harder for a bear to get a free meal, you are improving its odds of living a long and happy life—no matter what that hungry bear might think about it.

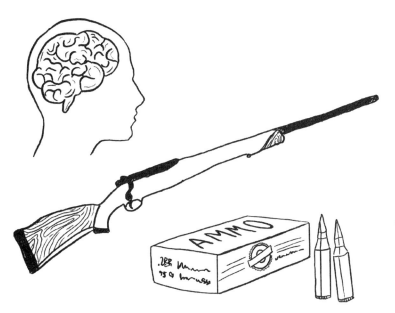

Human brain, hunting rifle, and ammo: When you encounter a bear, one of the depicted is more important than the other two. Use it.

RAPTORS, FERAL DOGS, AND ERMINES

Raptors—also known as birds of prey—include everything from owls, to red kites, to hawks, condors, and eagles. I have seen eagles grab wild ducks, and hawks grab chickens. They are adept at stealth: An owl's feathers are such that they fly silently. Just when you think you are at the top of the food chain, think again. If you can't outsmart an owl or an ermine, don't think *you* are at the top of the food chain, or if you are losing any type of livestock on a homestead, just know that the predator hunting your livestock is smarter than you. Period. If you don't believe me, ask that chicken that is no longer there. As far as that chicken is concerned, you: dumb, ermine: smart. Why did the chicken cross the road? To find a safer homestead. Egg-xactly.

Ermines have long, thin bodies and are notorious for being able to chew their way through chicken wire, creating a small hole that they can squeeze through. Once inside, they will kill the chickens for fun, partially eat them, and eat any eggs in the roosting box. On a recent homestead build, Matt constructed a chicken coop that was both ermine- and bear-proof. To do this, he used two layers of wire fencing: a heavier-duty chicken wire that was too sturdy for the ermines to gnaw through, and an even heavier-weight wire that would repel bears. As we said earlier in the livestock chapter, your chickens are safer the more contained they are. On this homestead, there were simply too many predators for the chickens to be allowed out of their small, heavily fortified run. Probably not the birds' first choice, but the only good choice for the homeowners.

While we were talking to these homesteaders, they shared that wild dogs were a problem in their area (Arizona). In fact, to prevent wild dogs from digging in to get the chickens (a growing problem in many areas), Matt dug two feet down, creating a wire apron around the coop in the ground that would stop even the most determined digger. In some areas feral dogs are dependent on humans both for food and for the "recruitment" of new abandoned dogs into the pack. If you see wild dogs near your property, take them seriously: Keep your pets inside or under your watch, secure your trash, and make sure there's nothing they want to eat in the compost pile.

— FOURTEEN —

THE
INGENIOUS
HOMESTEADER

Over the last nine seasons of filming, we have met some truly inspiring homesteaders, and one thing that always impresses me is a homesteader who is able to salvage old scrap and society's castoffs and build farming, construction, and homesteading equipment from things that other people label "junk." One man's pollution is another man's solution. No one, and I mean *no one*, does this better than my aforementioned friend Dave, a homesteader who lives a short drive from the forty and has, over his homesteading life, exemplified the old adage "reduce, reuse, recycle." Dave epitomizes the rugged, resilient determination that is the cornerstone of successful homesteading, especially in a place as difficult to homestead in as Alaska. As it turns out, it's in his blood—and maybe yours.

> ## One man's pollution is another man's solution.

THE HOMESTEADER LINEAGE

What do ninety-three million people in America (and very likely you . . .) have in common with Abraham Lincoln? Well, when Abraham Lincoln signed the Homestead Act of 1862, Alaska was nowhere to be found in his legislation. It wasn't until 1898, when President William McKinley expanded the program to include the territory of Alaska, that Alaskans too became eligible to file for 160-acre homesteads. Those who did file learned quickly there was no tougher place on earth than Alaska to homestead. By 1940, less than one thousand people had applied for a homestead in Alaska, even as four million homestead claims were filed in the Lower 48. Today, ninety-three million people are direct descendants of those original Lower 48 homesteaders, and make no mistake about it, these folks are tough and resilient. Most of these ninety-three million have grandparents who lived through a decade-long period (1930 to 1940) of droughts, dust storms, parched soils, winds, lack of rain, no jobs, and a devastating economy: the Dust Bowl.

Many people died, some starving to death. You've heard it said that when times get tough you may have to tighten your belt? The Dust Bowl was so tough that people thought about *eating* their belts. Then, with the tightening grip of the Great Depression, it truly became survival of the fittest. Just outside of Billings, Montana, Henry Hanson and his wife, Esther, were struggling to survive. Years later he remarked, "When you can't even grow three blades of grass in three years' time, it's time to go." And go he did. Far. He headed north to Alaska in 1939, before the army built the Alaska Highway. Henry made his way to Alaska first by steamship from Seattle to Seward. When he finally made it to the Matanuska Valley, he had six dollars to his name.

Back in 1975, I caught a ferry from Ketchikan to Haines, Alaska, looking for work. I slept in a ditch alongside the road (no sleeping bag) between the ferry terminal and the town of Haines. I was hungry, and down to one ten-dollar bill to my name. I bought a hamburger and fries, and after some deliberation, left a two-dollar tip. Yep. I was down to less money than Henry Hanson. Fortunately a man named John Schnabel (beloved character on the show *Gold Rush*) gave me a job, and I worked for him off and on for three years in his sawmill and logging operations. I also found an extremely remote off-grid log cabin sitting on a 160-acre homestead. Paradise. Life was good. I was newly wed, and once I got established, I sent for Mollee in Ketchikan.

Likewise, Henry and Esther Hanson found a large, inaccessible piece of unclaimed ground that had several springs on it and filed for a homestead. To qualify for a homestead you needed to live on site in an adequately built home for five years and clear twenty acres of land for agricultural purposes. No tents allowed. The Hansons' first home was a Quonset hut, an army surplus storage building they purchased for fifty dollars. They began to clear land, and once again the couple from Bemidji, Minnesota, by way of Montana, started over in the majestic Matanuska Valley, Alaska.

News of their adventurous life in mountainous Alaska made its way via letters back to the flat lands of Bemidji, where their seventeen-year-old nephew David Newcomb was becoming more and more interested in everything Alaska. A Minnesota farm boy, Dave grew up in the garden and credits his father for teaching him basic gardening skills from infancy that he would still be practicing long after his own retirement.

Dave was not your average seventeen-year-old kid, unless you know one who works two jobs, saves a hundred dollars to buy an old Ford delivery van, rebuilds its six-cylinder motor, and then puts it in gear pointing it due north. The destination? Wild Alaska, 3,250 rugged miles away. Alone. Exactly. In 1967, Dave (the eldest of six kids) left Minnesota, with his parents and siblings waving goodbye in the rearview mirror of his newly rebuilt van. Serendipitously, 1967 was also the year Alaska adopted the slogan, "North to the Future."

One adventurous week later, the heavy-duty delivery truck was a mere twenty-five miles from Uncle Henry's homestead. But then, one of his front "Maypop" (may pop at any time) tires blew out, sending the heavy vehicle off the road careening into the wild. This is a dangerous section of mountainous road, and four people that I knew personally have died on this very stretch of the Glenn Highway. The Ford flipped onto its side and skidded off into the tundra. Fortunately, Dave (and his Ford) dodged a bullet. A shaken Dave found someone down at King Mountain Lodge with a wrecker, and they managed to upright the vehicle, put on a new tire, and send Dave on down the last few miles of his journey. To think, Dave could have died in the last 25 miles of his 3,250-mile journey, less than an hour from his aunt and uncle's homestead.

THE SOUL OF A HOMESTEADER

Today, Dave still lives on that Hanson homestead, and perseverance lives on, generationally. Henry and Esther are long gone, but their spirit of adventure, hard work, ingenuity, problem-solving, and persistence endures. Just like his aunt and uncle, staring down the Depression and the Dust Bowl, Dave has seen good and bad times. The one thing he has never seen is a situation so difficult or so bad that it would make him want to quit.

Dave and his wife have one of the most successful homesteading farms I've seen, growing organic tomatoes, cucumbers, peppers, garlic, greens, and potatoes that they sell in the Anchorage Farmers Market during the (short) growing season. To make the most of these brief months, Dave has built a heated greenhouse out of huge clear plastic panels, recycled from a closing business, that he sourced from California and constructed into a large, peaked-roof building. He has a row of plastic-sheeted, commercial-size greenhouses, one of which he designed and built himself, again out of castoffs. His small garden by his house is made up of raised beds—all comfortably at waist height, to make tending to them easier, and all made out of recycled and reclaimed wood. Another garden area has raised beds that utilize decommissioned army cots for the framework of the beds. Dave's composter is two huge black cylindrical bins (recycled), elevated on posts to keep them out of the way of bears, that he rotates every day with a car battery–powered motor that he designed and built himself. Once the compost is ready to use, he uses a repurposed cement mixer, with a large cylindrical sieve fixed to the open end, to shift and sort the compost into the finer grade soil required for planting. His house is heated by a pressurized water system he also designed and built himself (don't try this at home, kids).

Raised garden beds
for convenience.

Dave designed and built his own sawmill (impressive), helped me build our one-of-a-kind log splitter for the forty (invaluable when we had to cut four cords of wood in two days to replace the logs that burned in the house fire), and is our go-to guy for any time we need to get creative. A few years back we designed and built the portable hydroelectric wheel for another local family in Alaska, as seen on *Homestead Rescue.*

Before he turned to homesteading full time, he was a welder, a construction guy, and a gold miner who also worked on tunneling projects for the state. The point is not so much to copy this level of creativity and skill, but more to understand that part of homesteading is always going to be looking at other people's castoffs and seeing resources instead of waste. Many homesteaders are frugal for the simple reason that they come from generations of people who were down to six dollars in their pockets. Even if times are good, you need to spend sparingly, keeping one eye open for that future when times might just be bad again. In keeping with this philosophy, many established homesteaders have an area of their property for "stuff." To the untrained eye, this can sometimes look like, well, junk. Piles of lumber, windows, and old doors scavenged from torn-down buildings. Old cars or obsolete equipment. Bicycles. In reality, these storage zones are the homesteaders' equivalent of Lowe's or Home Depot: invaluable resources of materials. We have our own store of materials, many of which come from members of the local community who know that we will make the most of scrap lumber—for instance—that they don't have use for and don't want to toss out.

Ever heard the expression "One man's trash is another man's treasure"? Well, when the first man mentioned here wears out a set of four truck tires, he loads 'em up and heads to the dump. However, our second man (or woman) sees those same worn-out tires as a potential planter to raise potatoes in. Or perhaps a set of landscaping stairs. How about a retaining wall? And this, folks, is "wear" the rubber meets the road. Ingenuity. Some old salvaged, weathered barnwood can actually bring a higher price than brand-new wood from the lumber store. Too often it too ends up in a landfill next to a set of four . . . potato planters. It's estimated that five hundred million tons of construction and demolition debris ends up in our landfills annually, and one (alarming) study said that this number could double by the year 2025. Yes, these statistics are concerning, but they can also be motivating. The more resourceful we become, the healthier our planet will become. And as Bob Barker would say, "The price is right!" So, think of recycling as *free*cycling and repurposing as *free*purposing. Who wouldn't want to save money AND help the environment at the same time? And speaking of pollution, who wouldn't want to be part of the solution? The more one's thinking adapts toward a simpler, scaled-down lifestyle, he or she incrementally will become more adept in their ingenuity. Thinking outside of the (trash) box.

Just like that younger Dave Newcomb adapted to the many challenges facing him on his now successful Alaskan homestead. If necessity is the mother of invention, ingenuity is the mother of original thought. I didn't reinvent the wheel, but I did mount two (bicycle) wheels at each side of the river on our tram towers, repurposing them as rope pulleys to pull our river tram car back and forth. To homestead is to be clever. To be clever is to invent. To invent is to create. And remember. Your brain has one hundred billion neurons ready to be clever, inventive, and creative. OK. Let's get a few neurons fired up.

FIFTEEN

WHEN IT ALL GOES WRONG

Preparation is key to successful homesteading. Over the last nine seasons, as Matt and Misty and I have traveled the country, we've spread the word about the importance of both planning and preparation. Planning means doing your research, investigating the good and the bad of different potential properties, anticipating the challenges you might face, and ensuring you are ready to deal with them. If you've planned well, you'll understand the risks that are typical for your area—maybe floods, maybe drought— and have both the knowledge and supplies that you need to survive these situations.

There are, however, some things you can't plan for, and this is where the preparation comes in. No one anticipated a pandemic, but some were better *prepared* to meet it. Well-prepared homesteaders were not anxious about food shortages. They knew that between their canned goods, crops, livestock, and root cellar, they would have food. Likewise, few people expected the catastrophic floods and fires of the recent years. But homesteaders who had elevated their homes (like our friends in Missouri, whose cabin is raised off of the ground by boulders) or built in fire resilience fared better than those who didn't plan for those worst-case scenarios.

I learned the hard way about the need to be prepared for the impossible myself in the fall of 2020, when, unbelievably, the worst-case scenario came a-calling. In early November that year, I developed a runny nose, sore throat, and headache and lost my sense of smell. Now, I'd been traveling for the show, and despite all the precautions, it seemed likely that I had COVID. Sure enough, I tested positive. A few days later Mollee manifested those same symptoms and tested positive. She developed a serious cough that, thankfully, subsided the day I was going to take her to the clinic.

For nine days we were both extremely lethargic and nonproductive. For maybe the first time in my life, I spent a lot of time just sitting in a cabin. Midmonth, a mild cold snap settled in and nightly temperatures were dipping below zero. I woke up on day ten of my infection and began the COVID-induced ritual, ambling zombie-like downstairs (from the sleeping loft) to sit dormant in the dark until daylight. Sunrise came with Mollee making her way to the kitchen, turning on the taps, and . . . nothing. She turned to me and said, "The water's frozen."

That's my cue, so I got up out of my stupor and walked over to our cabin's only heating source, a forty-year-old woodstove that was smoldering away. The house had gotten so cold overnight that our water line had frozen inside the house, most likely at a point farthest away from the woodstove's slowly waning heat. I grabbed Mollee's hair dryer, reached round the back of our three-hundred-gallon water storage, and pointed it at a suspect water line. A few minutes of hot blowing air will usually fix this problem, but not this time.

I realized that it must be a little colder than I thought in the house, so my next plan was to load the woodstove with dry spruce logs and generate some serious heat. An hour later the cabin was much warmer, but the water was still frozen. No problem: I continued adding dry spruce logs and the woodstove raged as the cabin got warmer. However, sitting there next to it I saw a wisp of smoke hovering in the kitchen area (keep in mind, we could not smell any smoke as we had lost our sense of smell with COVID). Strange. I got up from my seat and walked around the cabin, trying to make sense of this. A minute later I saw another small wisp of smoke waft out where the chimney pipe entered the ceiling. Not good. I immediately sensed the worst, pulled off the metal trim ring attached to the ceiling, and . . . saw the worst. The extreme heat from the stove had compromised the insulated chimney pipe, and all I could see was dense smoke and fire. I yelled out to Mollee to grab the fire extinguishers, and the battle to save the cabin began.

Of course, the act of discovering the fire had in itself made everything worse. Now with the chimney exposed, more air could feed the fire as it raced up to the peak of the roof between the rafters. I exhausted one fire extinguisher, and then another, filling the cabin with smoke and powder. By now small chunks of burning debris were falling down on top of the woodstove, adding to the smoke. I scraped them off onto the floor, still burning, knowing full well that time was running out. One last-ditch effort: I yelled for Mollee to bring me a chainsaw. Standing on a chair, I reached over my head and started to cut through the pine board ceiling to chase down the fire. It was burning somewhere between the rafters. Maybe. By now there are several smoke alarms beeping and the raging buzz of a chainsaw cutting away at the roof. Over the din, Mollee calls 911. Remember: We live off-grid, across a roaring river, with no road access. I've cut as high as I can reach overhead with a chainsaw, tip-toeing on top of a metal bar stool, and there's still more fire. I shout for another fire extinguisher, but Mollee shouts, "We're out!!" I yell back, "Then get me some water!" But as I was shouting those four words, it hit me. All the water lines in the house were still frozen solid. We had a three-hundred-gallon tank that could put out this fire in a moment, but we couldn't access it.

Right then and there, at that second, it hit me that our house might burn down before our very eyes. I didn't concede. I ran outside to take apart a twenty-foot extension ladder, allowing me to get higher inside the house than the bar stool would allow. I could continue cutting away at the burn and actually save the house. Every millisecond mattered, literally, and all of this was taking place with us both in an acute and confusing COVID mental fog. Frenzy. I found the twenty-foot extension ladder under two feet of snow and began trying to separate the ten-foot section. It was frozen. I began pounding the ice with my fists to no avail, then kicking at it with my boots. Futile. I decided to use the entire twenty-foot ladder to access the roof from outside the house, attacking the fire from the top. As I climbed up and onto the roof, I saw a significant area of metal roofing rippling and contorting from the heat immediately below it, succumbing to the extreme heat. We were losing the battle. I'd only been outside a few minutes, but when I went back in, the smoke was ten times worse. Defeated, I looked at Mollee and said, "Darlin', we're gonna watch our home burn to the ground." A few minutes later we got billowing smoke and flames. Mollee frantically rounded up Little Su and our cat, Baby, and ran for safety.

In retrospect, COVID's mind-altering effects, brain fog, and shock were affecting our decisions. We walked by original paintings, Alaskan artifacts, all my guns, a dozen instruments, and a lifetime sum of all our earthly possessions without saving them. Even the chainsaw that she brought in from outside went up in flames.

A few minutes later Miles showed up, after I had conceded defeat. He said we should try to save the woodstove. What woodstove? The brand-new one I had purchased on the showroom floor of the building supply store. It was sitting inside the cabin's front entry, ready to install, but COVID came, and the woodstove replacement would have to wait until I had the energy. The fact was that I was well aware that our old woodstove was dangerous, that it would burn too hot and potentially cause problems. Because of this I purchased this brand-new, and very expensive, stove that had all the required safety technologies (i.e., your chimney will never get dangerously hot). Miles and I wrestled with the heavy stove until we reached a safe distance from the burning house. As the burn picked up speed, I heard fire trucks in the distance and felt true sorrow for poor Mollee, standing there in below-zero temperatures, wearing the only material things she had left in the world: a pair of jeans, boots, a shirt, and a jacket.

Then: *BOOM!!!* "STAND BACK!" I shouted to all as a propane bottle exploded. I went back into that burning house, crawling on my hands and knees under the thickest, hottest smoke I'd ever seen, found five or six photo albums, and crawled back out for the last time. And then we did indeed stand there in below-zero temperatures and watch our home burn to the ground.

THE WORST-CASE SCENARIO

At some point in your homesteading life you will experience the worst-case scenario. For me and Mollee, it was a combination of COVID, a cold snap, and an old stove that I knew I needed to replace. For some of the homesteading families we've worked with over the years, it's been Mother Nature throwing them a curveball with hundred-year floods that are suddenly five-year floods. Others have been destabilized by the death of a matriarch or patriarch, kids who need to move away to find work, predators who are getting more aggressive and territorial, once-reliable crops that no longer thrive, or pretty much any unanticipated event. Here's the thing. If you've done the work we've talked about, buying land that has the best possible chance of surviving floods or fires, building a property elevated out of the way of danger, securing your livestock from hungry neighbors, you are exponentially better equipped to handle unforeseen occurrences, whatever and whenever that might be.

BEHIND THE SCENES

On the night of the day we lost *everything* in the fire, we spent our first homeless night in Misty and Maciah's cabin realizing we, in fact, had *everything* that we needed. Every member of the family had provided us with housing, food, and clothing (thanks, family). The very next morning before sunrise, I was determined to resume work on the far-from-finished log cabin on top of the cliff. Our family began chipping away at the glacier that was blocking the trail to the unfinished cabin with hand tools (thank you, Miles and family). It took until dark at below-zero temperatures before the road was passable to the top of the cliff (with a snowmachine). But then we discovered that, due to a recent wind storm, the last section of trail to the cabin was blocked by not one, but two massive spruce trees that had blown down in the storm. By now it was completely dark outside and to be honest, I was still weak from

COVID and a bit disheartened that after a full day of working, we still hadn't made it to our cabin build site. However, Matt encouraged me to walk with him the remaining thousand feet to the cabin, retrieve a chainsaw, and cut these trees out of the way to accomplish our mission. With the trees out of the way, we both jumped on the snowmachine and rode to the cabin site (thanks, Matt). It was a cold, tough day. But, in life, these are the days you remember—these are the days that can make you, or break you. The next morning, with a trail set in, we started over with nothing, and . . . *everything*.

FINAL NOTE

Since I began writing this in early 2021, there has been a cyberattack on a gas line, affecting millions of people across several states. Multiple COVID-19 variants have proven themselves nasty superspreaders, especially in large, crowded cities. Gas prices have soared to well over five dollars a gallon in California as inflation hits a thirty-one-year high. Food prices are skyrocketing, and grocery store shelves are once again looking bare as supply chains fracture.

Currently, 170 container ships are anchored offshore at just *one* port in Long Beach, California, awaiting their turn to be unloaded. Once they are unloaded, the trucking industry can't deliver the mountains of offloaded dockside shipping container goods due to yet another shortage: truck drivers.

This seems like the tip of the iceberg, and if it is, then 90 percent of the 'berg is looming unseen beneath the surface. But as the RMS *Titanic* can attest, the danger is still there.

The 883-foot-long ship was designed and built to carry 3,320 passengers. Famously, it only had lifeboat seating for 1,178. Not good. Everyone knew the ship was in iceberg-laden waters, but for some unknown reason the captain and crew pushed the 52,310-ton ship full-speed ahead. That's 104 million pounds. Pedal to the metal.

Yes, I'm going to go there.

It feels like we are "all aboard" our own 100-million-pound, twenty-first-century *Titanic*, going much faster than we should be, in dangerously troubled waters, carrying way too much baggage, and with far too little room on the lifeboats for all our passengers. At the prow of the ship, the passengers are pointing wide-eyed and straight ahead over the bow toward the obvious tip of an iceberg, shouting, "Look out!!!" Yet our leaders dismiss the outcry, increase the (unsinkable?) ship's speed, and command us to go out and put a fresh coat of paint on the mast. All the while, over the loudspeaker we hear: "We've got everything under control."

It's hard to see disaster coming, and it's even harder to accept its arrival. After the *Titanic* slammed into the iceberg, beautiful chunks of bluish glacier ice slid across the (already sinking) ship's deck, prompting some to fetch crystal glasses, fill them with champagne, and drop in some of that crystal clear ice(berg). The blissful ignorance lasted half an hour or so. Today, our "passengers" put their full confidence in their modern-day captains and crews, while blissfully continuing to "Eat, drink, and be merry . . ." It would be wise to remember the second half of Epicurus's famous saying: ". . . for tomorrow we may die."

Every single homesteader I've met has seen some facet of that iceberg's tip and has made a deliberate choice to cut loose a lifeboat and manifest their own destiny. Including me. And come the next cyberattack on the power grid, or food shortage due to a broken supply chain, or natural disaster such as a hurricane, flood, ice storm, drought, or earthquake, these homesteaders will fare far better than the less prepared, procrastinating, crowded masses.

How? These homesteaders have each developed their own independent water system, be it a drilled well, natural spring, or rain catchment. They've engineered their own "grid-free" power system, be it solar, wind, or hydro, and they've planted productive gardens, greenhouses, and orchards that provide healthy, organic foods.

Before we get off the *Titanic* tirade, let's remember the eight musicians who played on while the ship was sinking, calming the frightened passengers. Very, very noble. They played right up to the end and then "went down" in history as heroes.

As a musician myself, I can almost understand their thinking, but, come on. Who in their right mind wouldn't be thinking about their immediate surrounding circumstances and taking action toward self-preservation? Or perhaps seizing that precious little time to help others survive? These touchstone tales from the *Titanic* serve as historical, poignant, real-life reminders that people, then and now, often refuse to accept their reality until it is too late to do anything to change it. Although we all read the same headlines of the day, it seems most people can't see the forest for the trees, but I'm hoping that *you* can, and that you choose to FLEE to the forest and the trees.

If I only sold one copy of this book to one person, or one couple, or one family, who then used this book as a compass, pointing toward a better life: mission accomplished.

Throughout the nine seasons of *Homestead Rescue*, I have witnessed the positive trans-formation of men, women, couples, and families as they deliberately pursue a better life for themselves. And honestly, had it not been for their adventurous spirit, their fervor to live freely, and their tenacity to triumph in spite of unpredictable adversities, I most likely would not have been inspired to share their stories here with hopes of helping others to seek that same path to freedom and self-reliance.

Many reading this are in a rut. But here's the thing about ruts: If they get deep enough, they resemble a grave. How can you get out of a rut? Take risks. Make changes. Act. Shift. Transform. Innovate. Advance. As James Bryant Conant once said, "Behold the turtle. He makes progress only when he sticks his neck out." Tens of millions of people, for as many reasons, are making a change in their thinking and their lifestyles. *They* are from every walk of life, running toward a certain freedom and peace of mind found only in the moun-tains, deserts, and plains and along the coastlines—anywhere and everywhere there is less pavement, people, concrete, and congestion. In these last six months since I wrote and delivered this book to the publisher, it has been sobering to watch worldly trends and global events

Take risks. Make changes. Act.

lead us all down a very dangerous path. Cyberattacks on the grid, water, food supplies, transportation, and banks are inevitable. War has broken out. The world is on edge. What will the next six months bring?

I want to be optimistic, but I have to be realistic. Bad days are here. Worse days are com-ing. I've deliberately avoided pushing or aligning myself (or these pages) with any exhaust-ing political narratives. I don't need to. You know why there's an urban exodus. You know why there's an urban escape. You also know why there's never been a better time than right now to pursue self-reliance, self-sufficiency, independence, and freedom.

In a world that is living far too dangerously, make your choice: to live simply.

ACKNOWLEDGMENTS

I t is often said (and written) about founders of hugely successful companies and high-profile businesses that said founders are "self-made men." I'm here to say—there are *no* self-made men. Not *one*. Anywhere. Why? Because that "self-made man" most likely had an influential mother and father—or perhaps a prodigious sister or brother. Twelve years of primary and secondary education put him in close contact with many caring, dedicated teachers. Postsecondary education leads to even more potential mentors. By the time he enters the workforce, ALL of the above have contributed some unique measure of fuel to the fire that has forged the lone man he sees in the mirror. Perhaps in that very order. But a better man looks into that mirror and sees them *all*. I'm certainly not comparing myself to anyone of prominence, as I'm well aware that without all of the above you wouldn't be holding a book written by . . . us.

Nine seasons of *Homestead Rescue* required that I travel across North America helping homesteaders, leaving Mollee alone on our forty-acre, off-grid homestead that has no road access—in wild Alaska. She never complained. Misty and Matt were right there loyally at my side year after year, making extreme sacrifices, as their families couldn't make it to every episode to visit. However, that all changed as Season One of *Raney Ranch* fired up right here in Alaska, on our own homestead. Misty, her husband, Maciah, and their son, Gauge, built a log home of their own on the forty-acre spread. Melanee, her husband, Ari, and their three children, Mia, Col, and Taz, came to the homestead daily, contributing an army of labor and knowledge. Matt, his wife, Katie, and their son, Indy, worked alongside Miles, helping Mollee and me rebuild a new log home on top of the cliff, well aware that their parents were homeless after losing everything they owned in the cabin fire. Thank you, family.

Not long ago my agent, Jamie Young, contacted me about doing this project with Andrew Stuart, a book agent. Marian Lizzi, VP and editor in chief of TarcherPerigee at Penguin Random House, believed the premise to be timely and gave it a green light. Once Discovery came on board, it was time to set sail. Caroline Greeven guided me through the process. And last but certainly not least, my assistant in Alaska, Kelly Kuzina—an Alaskan high school English teacher with twelve years of college (straight A's since kindergarten), integral in my more than one hundred hours of TV, who knows I'm more adept at wielding a chainsaw than I am with a pen—made sure my *i*'s were dotted and my *t*'s were crossed.

And although only *one* face graces this book's cover, I'm humbly reminded of the impactive sum of all those mentioned, and how each and every last one (unwittingly) played their respective roles in getting me to this very "pen point" in time. I thank you all.

ABOUT THE AUTHOR

Marty Raney is the host of *Homestead Rescue*, a television show that in its ninth season has reached global success on Discovery. Marty also hosts another Discovery spin-off of *Homestead Rescue*, *Raney Ranch*, which follows the Raney family's off-grid life in Alaska. Over the last decade, Marty has logged more than one hundred hours of television.

Marty Raney's off-grid life began in North Bend, Washington. At age sixteen, he quit school, left home, and ventured to Alaska. Marty married Mollee Roestel and their off-grid Alaskan adventures began in 1974 in the logging camps of southeast Alaska. They later ventured eight hundred miles farther north to Southcentral Alaska, where the two, now with four children in tow, began hiking, skiing, subsistence hunting and fishing, and adventuring the vast wilderness of Alaska as a family.

Mountains have always played a significant role in Marty's Alaskan life. In 1986, he began guiding twenty-one-day climbing expeditions up North America's highest peak, Denali (elevation: 20,310 feet). To date, the Raneys are the only family of six (husband, wife, and four children) who have all climbed Denali multiple times. Marty reflects on his well-lived life in Alaska: "Some people have an adventure of a lifetime; in Alaska, I've had a lifetime of adventure."

After nearly forty-nine years in the forty-ninth state, Marty's beginnings have come full circle: The Raneys once again live off-grid with no road access. Marty and Mollee have carved out a piece of the Alaskan wilderness, living on a forty-acre homestead in Alaska, on property only accessible by crossing a torrential Class IV river. Their self-sustaining life in one of the harshest climates adheres to Marty's motto: "Alaska is better than fiction."